ORDO

for the Celebration of Mass according to *Divine Worship: The Missal*
and the Liturgy of the Hours according to *Divine Worship: Daily Office*
for the Personal Ordinariate of the Chair of Saint Peter

Advent 2023 to Christmastide 2024

According to the Particular Calendar
of the Personal Ordinariate of the Chair of Saint Peter,
coordinated with the National Calendars of the United States and Canada
issued by authority of the United States Conference of Catholic Bishops
and the Canadian Conference of Catholic Bishops

CONTENTS

IN the worship and service of Almighty God, which Christ and His Apostles have left to us, we are vouchsafed means, both moral and mystical, of approaching God, and gradually learning to bear the sight of Him. . . . We approach, and in spite of the darkness, our hands, or our head, or our brow, or our lips become, as it were, sensible of the contact of something more than earthly. We know not where we are, but we have been bathing in water, and a voice tells us that it is blood. Or we have a mark signed upon our foreheads, and it spake of Calvary. Or we recollect a hand laid upon our heads, and surely it had the print of nails in it, and resembled His who with a touch gave sight to the blind and raised the dead. Or we have been eating and drinking; and it was not a dream surely, that One fed us from His wounded side, and renewed our nature by the heavenly meat He gave. Thus in many ways He, who is Judge to us, prepares us to be judged,— He, who is to glorify us, prepares us to be glorified, that He may not take us unawares; but that when the voice of the Archangel sounds, and we are called to meet the Bridegroom, we may be ready.

~ Saint John Henry Newman, "Worship, a Preparation for Christ's Coming,"
Parochial and Plain Sermons, Vol. 5, Sermon 1.

Particular Notes on the Liturgical Year of 2023-2024 for the Ordinariate

1. Upon the recommendation of the Governing Council on 9 June 2016, Bishop Lopes has decreed that the following Solemnities will be observed as **Holy Days of Obligation** in the Ordinariate of the Chair of Saint Peter:

- 8 December, Solemnity of the Immaculate Conception
  (of precept in the United States but not in Canada)
- 25 December, Solemnity of the Nativity of Our Lord Jesus Christ
- 1 January , Solemnity of Mary, the Holy Mother of God
- Thursday of the Sixth Week of Easter, Solemnity of the Ascension
  (kept on its traditional date forty days after Easter, nine days before Whitsunday)
- 15 August, Solemnity of the Assumption of the Blessed Virgin Mary
- 1 November, Solemnity of All Saints

2. Whenever 1 January, 15 August, or 1 November fall on a Saturday or a Monday, the precept to attend Mass is abrogated. Mass attendance is always obligatory on Christmas (25 December), the Solemnity of the Immaculate Conception (if observed on 8 December), and on the Solemnity of the Ascension. When the Second Sunday of Advent falls on December 8th, the Immaculate Conception is transferred to Monday, December 9th, but the obligation to attend mass does not transfer.

3. For the liturgical year of 2023-2024, the Solemnity of the Immaculate Conception falls on Thursday, December 8th, 2023, and is a Holy Day of Obligation. In calendar year 2024, the Solemnity is transferred to Monday, December 9th, 2024, but the obligation to attend mass is not transferred to Monday.

4. The Bishop further decreed that, within the Ordinariate, the Solemnity of the Epiphany will be celebrated on the Sunday between 2 January and 8 January and that the Solemnity of the Most Precious Body and Blood of Christ (Corpus Christi) will be observed on the second Sunday after Pentecost (in keeping with the Latin Rite dioceses of the United States and Canada and per the determinations of the Episcopal Conferences of both countries).

5. In 2024, since the Solemnity of the Epiphany of the Lord is celebrated on Sunday, 7 January, the Feast of the Baptism of the Lord is celebrated on Monday, 8 January.

6. The Ordinariate's Solemnity of Title, the Solemnity of the Chair of Saint Peter, will be celebrated on its calendar date, Thursday 22 February, 2024, taking precedence over the Lenten Weekday.

7. The 2024 Chrism Mass for the Ordinariate will be celebrated by the Bishop at the Cathedral of Our Lady of Walsingham on Thursday, 21 March, which is Thursday in Passion Week. This is to accommodate the travel schedules of the clergy, allowing them to return to their parishes for Holy Week.

8. The Solemnity of the Annunciation of the Lord is transferred to Monday, 8 April, in the week following the Easter Octave.

9. The Solemnity of Saint Joseph, Spouse of the Virgin Mary, is on its usual date, Tuesday, 19 March.

10. The Feast of Our Lady of Walsingham, 24 September, falls on a Tuesday this year. At the Cathedral of Our Lady of Walsingham, since its Solemnity of Title outranks the Sunday after Trinity, the Solemnity is transferred to Sunday, 22 September, beginning with EP1 on Saturday and concluding with EP2. Elsewhere in the Ordinariate, the Feast is observed on Tuesday, and EP1 is not observed.

General Notes, Norms, & Explanations for the Use of this Ordo

1. This Ordo outlines the celebration of Holy Mass in the Personal Ordinariate of the Chair of Saint Peter for each day of the ecclesiastical year according to *Divine Worship: The Missal* (Catholic Truth Society, 2015) and the Roman Eucharistic Lectionary in the Revised Standard Version, Second Catholic Edition (Ignatius Press, 2006). In conformity with the Rubrical Directory, Calendar, and particular rubrics of *Divine Worship: The Missal*, this Ordo has been compiled with due attention to the relevant norms of the *Institutio Generalis Missalis Romani* (*General Instruction of the Roman Missal* 2010), *Missale Romanum, Editio typica tertia* 2002 (*The Roman Missal*, English translation according to the Third typical edition, 2010), and the *Ordo Lectionum Missae, Editio typica altera* (*Order of Readings for Mass*, Second typical edition, 1981).

2. For each day of the year, liturgical observances for celebrating Mass are provided. Sundays and Solemnities are indicated by CAPITAL letters. The rank of each day's observance is given to the right (*Solemnity, Feast, Memorial*), except for Optional Memorials whose titles are indicated in *italics*.

3. The color of the liturgical vestments and antependia for each day's celebration is designated on the right hand side of each entry and is so indicated according to the norms laid out in *Divine Worship: The Missal*, Rubrical Directory, no. 43. The colors for Optional Memorials and alternative observances are given in *italic* type.

4. Observances proper to, or optional in, the United States are designated USA: whilst observances proper to, or optional in, Canada are designated Can: according to the Ordinariate's Particular Calendar and the relevant National Calendars issued by the USCCB and CCCB. Observances and their dates proper to the National Calendars which are not already inscribed in the Ordinariate's Particular Calendar are included in this Ordo and may be kept or not in the respective country according to pastoral needs and the custom of each community.

5. DWM = *Divine Worship: The Missal*. For each entry, DWM is followed by numbers referring to the pages of the Missal for the relevant Mass formularies and associated rites.

6. Lec = Roman Eucharistic Lectionary, RSV-2CE (2 volumes in the Ignatius Press edition). The citations may differ from the citations given in the *Ordo Lectionum Missæ* (1981) due to differing versification. For each entry, "Lec:" is followed by numbers referring to the section numbers of the Lectionary containing the readings at Mass as appointed or permitted for each day and observance. When alternative numbers or ranges of such numbers are given, appropriate readings should be selected from those provided in the Lectionary as suited to the rank and character of each Mass. The relevant Lectionary cycle is indicated before the entries for the beginning of Advent:

> **Sunday Cycle**: YEAR B (3 December 2023 to 24 November 2024)
>
> **Weekday Cycle**: CYCLE II (9 January 2024 to 13 February 2024 &
> 20 May 2024 to 30 November 2024)
>
> **Sunday Cycle**: YEAR C (1 December 2024 to 23 November 2025)

The cycles given above have been used in the preparation of this Ordo. The readings from the Proper of Time and Proper of Saints have been used for all Solemnities and all Feasts since they must take the place of the weekday readings for those respective days. The readings from the weekday cycle generally are to be used even on days on which a Memorial or Optional Memorial of a Saint occurs. The exceptions to this rule are those Memorials or Optional Memorials which have proper readings (usually only the Gospel) assigned to them in the Lectionary for Mass and which must be used on those days. Substitutions from the Commons or Proper of Saints may be made for the other readings suggested for those Memorials or Optional Memorials. The Priest Celebrant, however, should not omit "too often or without sufficient cause the readings assigned for each day in the Weekday Lectionary" (Introduction to the *Lectionary for Mass*, no. 83).

7. According to their kind and precedence, liturgical observances are to be celebrated at Mass as follows:

a) *Sundays*:   Except in Advent, Pre-Lent, and Lent, and on All Souls' Day when it falls on a Sunday, the Gloria is sung or said at each Mass, including anticipated Masses of the Sunday celebrated on Saturday evening.   Ordinarily, there are three assigned readings (Lesson, Epistle, and Gospel) for Sundays, aside from the Lectionary's Psalm or the Missal's Gradual, except as otherwise appointed. The Creed is said or sung, unless replaced by another form of the Profession of Faith (as when Baptism or Confirmation is administered during Mass, or as on Easter Sunday when the Renewal of Baptismal Promises may replace the Nicene Creed).

b) *Solemnities*:   The Gloria and the Creed are sung or said. The Lectionary appoints three proper readings (Lesson, Epistle, and Gospel), as indicated in this Ordo for each Solemnity. Some Solemnities have proper Vigil Masses appointed for celebration on the eve before the day, as indicated in this Ordo.

c) *Feasts*: The Gloria is said, but not ordinarily the Creed, for Feasts falling on weekdays. The Lectionary appoints two readings proper to each Feast, as specified in this Ordo.

d) *Memorials*: These are obligatory in character (as distinguished from Optional Memorials), unless impeded by a higher ranking celebration. The Gloria and the Creed are not said. For Memorials of Saints, the readings appointed in the *Lectio Continuo* for the weekdays are normally used as specified in this Ordo by the first listing for the day. In cases where there is pastoral benefit, readings selected from among the relevant Commons provided in the Lectionary may be used as indicated in this Ordo by the second, alternative listing for the day. However, proper readings assigned in the Lectionary for certain Memorials must be used instead of any *Lectio Continuo* or Commons readings. These are indicated in this Ordo in **bold**, and in the Lectionary by the specific reference "proper." Memorials that occur on the weekdays of Lent have the status of Optional Memorials and may be commemorated, if at all, only by the use of the Collect. The other Mass texts, readings, and the color for the celebration remain as specified for the weekdays of the Lenten season. Ember Days and Rogation Days have the status of Obligatory Memorials.

e) *Optional Memorials*: The Gloria and the Creed are not said. The readings typically follow the weekday *Lectio Continuo*. When readings for the memorial are provided, either explicitly or from the relevant commons, and when the pastoral benefit of the faithful commends the option, these may be used instead of the *Lectio Continuo*. However, where the Lectionary provides proper readings for a given Optional Memorial, indicated in **bold**, these must be used. Optional Memorials falling on the weekdays of Advent from 17 December to 24 December, on days in the Octave of Christmas, and on the weekdays of Lent have the status of "commemorations" and may be observed, if at all, only by the use of the Collect. In this Ordo, references to Memorials and Optional Memorials impeded by higher ranking celebrations are omitted or set apart in brackets [   ] when they can be kept as optional "commemorations" (using the Collect only at Mass with the other texts coming from the appointed Mass of the weekday). Otherwise, where such Memorials, thus bracketed, are impeded at Mass, the relevant Collects may be said as optional commemorations after the designated Collect of the Day at Morning and/or Evening Prayer.

f) *Feria*: Days designated as ferial take for their Mass formularies the texts assigned to the previous Sunday, or in some cases from the previous Solemnity, as appointed in the Missal and designated in this Ordo. Ferial days also permit the celebration of a coinciding Optional Memorial or a Mass of Saint Mary (on Saturdays), if so indicated, or of a Votive Mass or appropriate Mass for Various Needs and Occasions, in those times when such Masses are allowed. (*Divine Worship: The Missal* provides five Masses of Saint Mary, for celebration over the course of the liturgical year. As appointed to different times of the year, these constitute privileged Votive Masses and may be celebrated on unimpeded

Saturdays, even during Advent and Lent, when they are to be celebrated in violet vestments and with the appointed readings of the weekday.)

g) *Votive Masses, Masses for Various Needs and Occasions, Ritual Masses, and Masses for the Dead*: These Masses may be celebrated according to pastoral needs and for the benefit of the faithful, when allowed, according to the particular rubrics of the relevant Mass formularies in the Missal. See Appendix 4 of this Ordo for an outline of the occasions when the Mass texts of the day may be replaced with such Masses.

8) The symbol ¶ marks notes on special features of *Divine Worship: The Missal* which may be useful in liturgical planning and helpful in familiarizing clergy and those who assist with public worship with the distinctive character of this particular adaptation of the Roman Rite. These notes, however, are not exhaustive and do not substitute for acquired knowledge of the Missal's contents.

9) *Divine Office*: This Ordo includes citations for first and second Lessons at Morning and Evening Prayer for every day of the liturgical year, as found in *Divine Worship: Daily Office* (2020, Newman House Press). The Ordo also indicates a distribution of proper psalms for Morning and Evening Prayer each day. Alternatively, psalms may be read in sequence, over the course of each month, according to the traditional 30-day schema designated in the Psalter of *Divine Worship: Daily Office*. In addition, this Ordo indicates those days on which the *Te Deum* is said at Morning Prayer (most Sundays, Solemnities, and Feasts).

Abbreviations & Symbols

DWM = *Divine Worship: The Missal*
Lec =   Lectionary for Mass. Revised Standard Version, Second Catholic Edition (Ignatius Press, 2006)
HDO = Holy Day of Obligation
OT =   Ordinary Time (*Tempus per annum*)
MP =   Morning Prayer
EP =   Evening Prayer, with *EP 1* designating First Evensong and *EP 2* Second Evensong
Pss =   Psalm(s)

♦   separates the citation of Readings at Mass and of Lessons at the Divine Office:
First Reading (Lesson) ♦ Second Reading (Epistle) ♦ Gospel / First Lesson ♦ Second Lesson

¶   indicates references to special rubrics and texts of *Divine Worship* pertinent to the liturgical observance of the day, occasion, or season

❖   designates notes on certain liturgical norms and decisions particular to the Ordinariate of the Chair of Saint Peter as determined by the Bishop and his Governing Council

†   introduces entries in the Necrology of the Personal Ordinariate of the Chair of Saint Peter

♦   is also used on Sundays and Solemnities to separate the First Reading from the Citation for the Psalm in the 1928 Coverdale Psalter. This is a work in progress, undertaken to facilitate patrimonial Anglican Chant. The verses listed may differ from the verses in the responsorial psalm as given in the RSV-2CE lectionary due to any of the following: (a) inherent verse differences in the translations, (b) expansion to full verses to facilitate the use of Anglican Chant, (c) incorporation of the response as a verse, or (d) changes made to correspond to the more recent lectionary as used in other parishes of the Latin Church.

Ordo Missæ celebrandæ et Divini Officii persolvendi pro anno liturgico 2023-2024

December 2023

Lectionary Cycle:
Year B - Weekdays Year II - Daily Office Year II

3 SUN   FIRST SUNDAY OF ADVENT   Violet

DWM 152 Creed

Lec 2: Is 63:16d-17; 64:1,3b-8 ♦ Ps 80:1-3, 14-15, 17-19 ♦ 1 Cor 1:3-9 ♦ Mk 13:33-37

> ¶ The Litany may be sung in procession before the principal Sunday Mass (DWM 1061).
> ¶ The Advent Prose may be sung on any of the Sundays of Advent (DWM 151).

MP Pss: 146-147   Lessons: Is 1:1-20 ♦ Rv 14:13-15:4   Te Deum
EP 2   111-113   Is 2:10-end ♦ Jn 3:1-21

> ¶ *Alma Redemptoris Mater* may be said after EP or Compline from Advent through Candlemas.

4 Mon   Advent Feria   Violet
              Or:
              St John Damascene, Priest and Doctor of the Church   White

DWM 152

Lec 175: Is 2:1-5 ♦ Mt 8:5-11

  Or, for St John Damascene, Priest and Doctor of the Church: DWM 894

Lec 686: 2 Tm 1:13-14; 2:1-3 (#722.11) ♦ Mt 25:14-30 (#742.12)

MP Pss: 1-3   Lessons: Is 3:1-15 ♦ Mk 1:1-20
EP   4, 7   Is 4:2-end ♦ Rv 6

5 Tue   Advent Feria   Violet

DWM 152

Lec 176: Is 11:1-10 ♦ Lk 10:21-24

| MP | Pss: 5-6 | Lessons: | Is 5:1-17 ♦ Mk 1:21-end |
| EP | 10-11 | | Is 5:18-end ♦ Rv 7 |

6 Wed   Ember Wednesday in Advent   Violet
        [St Nicholas, Bishop]
DWM 154
Lec 177: Is 25:6-10a ♦ Mt 15:29-37
St Nicholas, Bishop may optionally be commemorated only in the Daily Office by adding the DWM 894 Collect after the Collect of the Day.

| MP | Pss: 119:I-III | Lessons: | Is 6 ♦ Mk 2:1-22 |
| EP | 12-14 | | Is 8:16-9:7 ♦ Rv 8 |

7 Thu   Saint Ambrose, Bishop and Doctor of the Church *Memorial*   White
DWM 895
Lec 178: Is 26:1-6 ♦ Mt 7:21, 24-27
    Or:
Lec 688: Eph 3:8-12 (#728.4) ♦ Jn 10:11-16 (#724.10)

MP	Pss: 18:I	Lessons:	Is 9:8-10:4 ♦ Mk 2:23-3:12
EP 1 of THE IMMACULATE CONCEPTION			
	Pss: 110, 113, 122	Lessons:	Sir 24:17-22 ♦ Rom 8:28-30

8 Fri   IMMACULATE CONCEPTION OF THE BLESSED VIRGIN MARY   White
    Solemnity HDO (Patronal Feastday of the USA)
DWM 896 Gloria, Creed
Lec 689: Gn 3:9-15, 20 ♦ Ps 98:1-5 ♦ Eph 1:3-6, 11-12 ♦ Lk 1:26-38

| MP | Pss: 63, 100 | Lessons: | Is 61:10-62:5 ♦ 1 Cor 1:26-30 | Te Deum |
| EP 2 | 45, 93 | | Zep 3:14-17 ♦ Rv 11:19, 12:1-6, 10 | |

> ¶ Today being a *Solemnity,* the obligation to abstain from meat or to perform some other penitential act is dispensed (CIC 1251).

9 Sat   Ember Saturday in Advent   Violet
        [St Juan Diego Cuauhtlatoatzin]
DWM 156
Lec 180: Is 30:19-21, 23-26 ♦ Mt 9:35-10:1, 5a, 6-8
St Juan Diego Cuauhtlatoatzin may optionally be commemorated only in the Daily Office by adding the DWM 897 Collect after the Collect of the Day.

December 2023

MP Pss: 20-21   Lessons: Is 13:1-14:2 ♦ Mk 4:1-20

EP 1 of The Second Sunday of Advent

      Pss: 110, 116-117   Lessons: Is 14:3-27 ♦ Rv 11

10 SUN   SECOND SUNDAY OF ADVENT   Violet

DWM 158 Creed

Lec 5: Is 40:1-5, 9-11 ♦ Ps 85:7-13 ♦ 2 Pt 3:8-14 ♦ Mk 1:1-8

MP Pss: 148-150   Lessons: Is 11:1-9 ♦ Rv 20:11-21:7   Te Deum

EP 2   114-115   Is 11:10-12:end ♦ Lk 1:1-25

11 Mon   Advent Feria   Violet

    Or:

    St Damasus I, Pope   *White*

DWM 158

Lec 181: Is 35:1-10 ♦ Lk 5:17-26

    Or, for St Damasus I, Pope: DWM 898

Lec 690: Acts 20:17-18a, 28-32, 36 (#720.2) ♦ Jn 15:9-17 (#724.11)

MP Pss: 25   Lessons: Is 17 ♦ Mk 4:21-end

EP   9, 15   Is 18 ♦ Rv 12

12 Tue   Our Lady of Guadalupe *Feast*   White

DWM 899 Gloria

Lec 690A: Zec 2:10-13 (#707.11), or Rv 11:19a; 12:1-6a, 10ab (#708.2) ♦ Lk 1:26-38 (#712.4), or Lk 1:39-47 (#712.5)

MP Pss: 24, 46   Lessons: Gn 12:1-7 ♦ Lk 11:27-28   Te Deum

EP   87, 95   Zec 2:1-13 ♦ Eph 1:3-12

13 Wed   Saint Lucy, Virgin and Martyr *Memorial*   Red

DWM 900

Lec 183: Is 40:25-31 ♦ Mt 11:28-30

    Or:

Lec 692: 2 Cor 10:17-11:2 (#734.2) ♦ Mt 25:1-13 (#736.2)

MP Pss: 38   Lessons: Is 21:1-12 ♦ Mk 5:21-end

EP   119:IV-VI   Is 22:1-14 ♦ Rv 14

14 Thu   Saint John of the Cross, Priest and Doctor of the Church *Memorial*   White

DWM 901

Lec 184: Is 41:13-20 ♦ Mt 11:11-15

    Or:

Lec 693: 1 Cor 2:1-10a (#728.2) ♦ Lk 14:25-33 (#742.23)

MP	Pss: 37:I	Lessons:	Is 24 ♦ Mk 6:1-13
EP	37:II		Is 28:1-13 ♦ Rv 15

15 Fri   Advent Feria   Violet
DWM 158
Lec 185: Is 48:17-19 ♦ Mt 11:16-19

MP	Pss: 31	Lessons:	Is 28:14-end ♦ Mk 6:14-29
EP	35		Is 29:1-14 ♦ Rv 16

16 Sat   Advent Feria   Violet
                Or:
                BVM: Mass of Saint Mary 1   *White*
DWM 158
Lec 186: Sir 48:1-4, 9-11b ♦ Mt 17:10-13
        Or, for Saint Mary: DWM 990
Lec 707-712 any readings from the Common of the BVM

MP	Pss: 30, 32	Lessons:	Is 29:15-end ♦ Mk 6:30-end
EP 1 of The Third Sunday of Advent			
	Pss: 42-43	Lessons:	Is 30:1-18 ♦ Rv 17

17 SUN   THIRD SUNDAY OF ADVENT [O Sapientia]   Rose/Violet
DWM 160 Creed
Lec 8: Is 61:1-2a, 10-11 ♦ Magnificat (DWDO 104-105) ♦ 1 Thes 5:16-24 ♦ Jn 1:6-8, 19-28

> ¶ "On the appointed days, these [Advent] Anthems following are sung or said before and after [as antiphons on] the *Magnificat* at Evening Prayer," beginning with *O Sapientia* on 17 December (DWM 162).

MP	Pss: 63, 98	Lessons:	Is 28:9-22 ♦ Rv 21:9-22:5	Te Deum
EP 2	103		Is 30:8-21 ♦ Mt 3	

18 Mon   18 December (O Adonai)   Violet
DWM 168
Lec 194: Jer 23:5-8 ♦ Mt 1:18-24

MP	Pss: 41, 52	Lessons:	Is 30:19-end ♦ Mk 7:1-23
EP	44		Is 31 ♦ Rv 18

19 Tue	19 December (O Radix Jesse)	Violet

DWM 170

Lec 195: Jgs 13:2-7, 24-25a ♦ Lk 1:5-25

MP	Pss: 45	Lessons: Is 38:1-20 ♦ Mk 7:24-8:10
EP	47-48	Is 40:1-11 ♦ Rv 19

20 Wed	20 December (O Clavis David)	Violet

DWM 172

Lec 196: Is 7:10-14 ♦ Lk 1:26-38

MP	Pss: 119:VII-IX	Lessons: Is 40:12-end ♦ Mk 8:11-9:1
EP	49, 53	Is 41 ♦ Rv 20

21 Thu	21 December (O Oriens)	Violet

[*St Peter Canisius, Priest and Doctor of the Church*]

DWM 174

Lec 197: Sg 2:8-14 or Zep 3:14-18a ♦ Lk 1:39-45

Or, for St Peter Canisius, Priest and Doctor of the Church: DWM 901 – if commemorated, Collect only

MP	Pss: 50	Lessons: Is 42:1-17 ♦ Mk 9:2-32
EP	33	Is 42:18-43:13 ♦ Rv 21:1-14

22 Fri	22 December (O Rex Gentium)	Violet

DWM 176

Lec 198: 1 Sm 1:24-28 ♦ Lk 1:46-56

MP	Pss: 40, 54	Lessons: Is 43:14-44:5 ♦ Mk 9:33-end
EP	51	Is 44:6-23 ♦ Rv 21:15-22:5

23 Sat	23 December (O Emmanuel)	Violet

[*St John of Kanty, Priest*]

DWM 178

Lec 199: Mal 3:1-4, 4:5-6 ♦ Lk 1:57-66

Or, for St John of Kanty, Priest: DWM 902 – if commemorated, Collect only

MP Pss: 55   Lessons: Is 44:24-45:13 ♦ Mk 10:1-31

EP 1 of The Fourth Sunday of Advent

Pss: 138-139   Lessons: Is 45:14-end ♦ Rv 22:6-end

24 SUN   FOURTH SUNDAY OF ADVENT [O Virgo Virginum]   Violet

DWM 164 Creed

Lec 11: 2 Sm 7:1-5, 8b-12, 14a, 16 ♦ Ps 89:1-4, 27, 29 ♦ Rom 16:25-27 ♦ Lk 1:26-38

MP Pss: 45-46   Lessons: Is 35 ♦ Rv 22:6-end   Te Deum
EP 1 of Christmas
     Pss: 89:I   Lessons: Zec 2:10-end ♦ Ti 2:11-3:7

> ¶ The Proclamation of the Nativity of Our Lord Jesus Christ "may be chanted or recited, most appropriately on 24th December, at Evening Prayer" (DWM 1069). Otherwise, the Proclamation may be made before the Christmas Mass during the Night.

25 Mon   NATIVITY OF THE LORD *Solemnity* HDO   White

Vigil Mass (Masses on Christmas Eve which begin before 10:00 PM)

DWM 184 Gloria, Creed

Lec 13: Is 62:1-5 ♦ Ps 89:1, 3-4, 16-17, 27, 29 ♦ Acts 13:16-17, 22-25 ♦ Mt 1:1-25 or 1:18-25

Mass In the Night (Masses on Christmas Eve which begin at 10:00 PM or later)

DWM 186 Gloria, Creed

Lec 14: Is 9:2-7 ♦ Ps 96:1-3, 11-13 ♦ Ti 2:11-14 ♦ Lk 2:1-14

> ¶ The Proclamation of the Nativity of Our Lord Jesus Christ may "be chanted or recited before the beginning of the Christmas Mass during the Night. It may not replace any part of the Mass" (DWM 1069).

Mass at Dawn (Masses on Christmas Day which begin before 9:00 AM)

DWM 188 Gloria, Creed

Lec 15: Is 62:11-12 ♦ Ps 97:1, 6, 11-12 ♦ Ti 3:4-7 ♦ Lk 2:15-20

Mass on the Day (Masses on Christmas Day which begin at 9:00 AM or later)

DWM 190 Gloria, Creed

Lec 16: Is 52:7-10 ♦ Ps 98:1-7 ♦ Heb 1:1-6 ♦ Jn 1:1-18 or 1:1-5, 9-14

> ¶ The Last Gospel "is especially appropriate in Christmastide, until the Baptism of the Lord or until Candlemas."
>
> ¶ Following the Mass During the Day, when the Prologue of John is the Gospel of the Mass, Lec 20: Matthew 2:1-12 may be read as the Last Gospel in place of the Prologue (DWM 1058).

MP Pss: 2, 85   Lessons: Is 9:2-7 ♦ Lk 2:1-20   Te Deum
EP 2   110, 132   Is 7:10-14 ♦ 1 Jn 4:7-end

26 Tue   Saint Stephen, the First Martyr *Feast*   Red

DWM 902 Gloria

Lec 696: Acts 6:8-10; 7:54-59 ♦ Ps 31:3-4, 6,8, 17-18 ♦ Mt 10:17-22

MP Pss: 28, 30   Lessons: Gn 4:1-10 ♦ Acts 6   Te Deum
EP   118   Ex 18:13-26 or Is 49:14-25 ♦ Acts 7:59-8:8

December 2023

27 Wed   Saint John, Apostle and Evangelist *Feast*   White
DWM 904 Gloria
Lec 697: 1 Jn 1:1-4 ♦ Ps 97:1-2, 5-6, 11-12 ♦ Jn 20:2-8

    MP Pss: 97-98   Lessons: Ex 33:9-19 ♦ Jn 13:21-35   Te Deum
    EP   145   Is 6:1-8 ♦ 1 Jn 5:1-12

28 Thu   Holy Innocents, Martyrs *Feast*   Red
DWM 905 Gloria
Lec 698: 1 Jn 1:5-2:2 ♦ Ps 124:1-4, 6-7 ♦ Mt 2:13-18

    MP Pss: 2, 26   Lessons: Jer 31:1-17 ♦ Mt 18:1-10   Te Deum
    EP   19, 126   Bar 4:21-27 or Gn 37:13-20 ♦ Mk 10:13-16

29 Fri   Fifth Day in the Octave of Christmas   White
          [*St Thomas Becket, Bishop and Martyr*]
DWM 190
Lec 202: 1 Jn 2:3-11 ♦ Lk 2:22-35
    Or, for St Thomas Becket, Bishop and Martyr: DWM 907 – if commemorated, Collect only

    MP Pss: 18:I   Lessons: Is 55 ♦ Jn 1:14-18   Te Deum
    EP   18:II   Is 60:1-12 ♦ Mt 11:2-6

30 Sat   Sixth Day in the Octave of Christmas   White
DWM 190
Lec 203: 1 Jn 2:12-17 ♦ Lk 2:36-40

    MP Pss: 20-21   Lessons: Is 60:13-end ♦ Jn 3:16-21   Te Deum
    EP 1 of The Holy Family
        Pss: 23, 27   Lessons: Nm 6:22-26 ♦ Lk 21:25-36

31 SUN   HOLY FAMILY OF JESUS, MARY AND JOSEPH *Feast*   White
DWM 192 Gloria, Creed
Lec 17: Gn 15:1-6; 21:1-3 or Sir 3:2-6, 12-14 ♦ Ps 105:1-9 or Ps 128:1-6 ♦ Heb 11:8, 11-12, 17-19 or Col 3:12-21 ♦ Lk 2:22-40 or 2:22, 39-40

> ¶ The first reading, psalm, and second reading from Year A may be used in Years B and C. The Gospel for each year is proper. The Year B readings are listed first in the citation above. In the RSV-2CE lectionary, the Year A first and second readings are given first, beginning on page 329, followed by the proper Gospel for Year B. The Year B readings, including a duplicate copy of the proper Gospel, begin on page 333 of the Lectionary. Sacristans and Readers should consult with the Celebrant or Homilist to ascertain the desired reading before setting the book and before reading.

MP Pss: 93, 96   Lessons: Is 41:8-20 ♦ Col 1:1-20   Te Deum

EP 1 of Mary, Mother of God

        Pss: 90   Lessons: Is 65:15b-25 ♦ Rv 21:1-6

January 2024

1 Mon   MARY, THE HOLY MOTHER OF GOD *Solemnity*   White
DWM 194 Gloria, Creed
Lec 18: Nm 6:22-27 ♦ Ps 67:1-2, 4-5, 7 ♦ Gal 4:4-7 ♦ Lk 2:16-21

> ¶ This year the Solemnity of Mary, the Holy Mother of God, falls on a Monday, and the obligation to attend Mass is abrogated.

MP Pss: 103	Lessons: Is 62:1-5,10-12 ♦ Rv	Te Deum
EP 2 148	19:11-16	
	Gn 17:1-12a,15-16 ♦ Mt 1:18-25	

2 Tue   Saints Basil the Great and Gregory Nazianzen, Bishops and Doctors of the   White
Church *Memorial*
DWM 661
Lec 205: 1 Jn 2:22-28 ♦ Jn 1:19-28
  Or:
Lec 510: Eph 4:1-7, 11-13 (#722.8) ♦ Mt 23:8-12 (#724.3)

| MP Pss: 34 | Lessons: Is 63:1-6 ♦ Mt 1:18-end |
| EP   33 | Is 63:7-end ♦ 1 Thes 1 |

3 Wed   Christmastide Feria (of The Second Sunday of Christmas)   White
  Or:
  The Most Holy Name of Jesus   *White*
DWM 196
Lec 206: 1 Jn 2:29-3:6 ♦ Jn 1:29-34
  Or, for The Most Holy Name of Jesus: DWM 662

| MP Pss: 68 | Lessons: Is 64 ♦ Mt 2 |
| EP   72 | Is 65:1-16 ♦ 1 Thes 2:1-16 |

4 Thu   Saint Elizabeth Ann Seton, Religious *Memorial*   White
DWM 663
Lec 207: 1 Jn 3:7-10 ♦ Jn 1:35-42

| MP Pss: 85, 87 | Lessons: Is 65:17-end ♦ Mt 3:1-4,11 |
| EP   89:I | Is 66:1-9 ♦ 1 Thes 2:17-3:end |

5 Fri   USA: Saint John Neumann, Bishop *Memorial*   White
  Can: Christmastide Feria   White
DWM (USA:) 664 (Can:) 196

Lec 208: 1 Jn 3:11-21 ♦ Jn 1:43-51

MP	Pss: 2, 110	Lessons: Is 66:10-end ♦ Mt 4:12-5:16
EP	29, 98	Is 42:1-9 ♦ 1 Thes 4:1-12

6 Sat   Christmastide Feria   White
Or:
BVM: Mass of Saint Mary 2   *White*
USA: *St André Bessette, Religious*   *White*
DWM 196
Lec 209: 1 Jn 5:5-13 ♦ Mk 1:7-11 or Lk 3:23-38 or Lk 3:23, 31-34, 36, 38
    Or, for Saint Mary: DWM 991
Lec 707-712 any readings from the Common of the BVM
    Or, for St André Bessette, Religious: DWM 665

MP	Pss: 46, 97	Lessons: Hos 2:14-3:end ♦ Mt 5:17-end
EP 1 of THE EPIPHANY		
	Pss: 66-67	Lessons: Is 42:1-9 ♦ Rom 15:8-21

7 SUN   EPIPHANY OF THE LORD *Solemnity*   White
DWM 198 Gloria, Creed
Lec 20: Is 60:1-6 ♦ Ps 72:1-2, 7-8, 10-13 ♦ Eph 3:2-3a, 5-6 ♦ Mt 2:1-12

> ¶ "On the Epiphany of the Lord, after the proclamation of the Gospel, a Deacon or cantor, in keeping with an ancient practice of Holy Church, announces from the ambo the moveable feasts of the current year" (DWM 1070).
> ❖ By decision of the Governing Council, ratified by the Bishop, the Solemnity of the Epiphany shall be celebrated on the Sunday between 2 January and 8 January, in keeping with the Latin Rite dioceses of the United States and Canada.

MP	Pss: 87, 93	Lessons: Is 49:1-13 ♦ Lk 3:15-22	Te Deum
EP 2	72	Is 60:9-end ♦ Jn 2:1-11	

8 Mon   Baptism of the Lord *Feast*   White
DWM 200 Gloria
Lec 21: Is 55:1-11 or Is 42:1-4, 6-7 ♦ Ecce Deus (DWDO 74) or Psalm 29:1-4, 9-10 ♦ 1 Jn 5:1-9 or Acts 10:34-38 ♦ Mk 1:7-11

> ¶ The first reading, psalm, and second reading from Year A may be used in Years B and C. The Gospel for each year is proper. The Year B readings are listed first in the citation above. In the RSV-2CE lectionary, the Year A first and second readings are given first, beginning on page 350, followed by the proper Gospel for Year B. The Year B readings, including a duplicate copy of the proper Gospel, begin on page 352 of the Lectionary. Sacristans and Readers should consult with the Celebrant or Homilist to ascertain the desired reading before setting the book and before reading.
>
> ¶ When the Baptism of the Lord is observed on Monday, only one of the two readings supplied is read before the Gospel.

MP Pss: 66	Lessons: Is 42:1-12 ♦ Jn 4:1-26 (27-42)	Te Deum
EP 42	Is 43:1-13 ♦ Jn 12:20-36a	

9 Tue Feria (of The Epiphany) (OT 1) *Green*
DWM 198
Lec 306: 1 Sm 1:9-20 ♦ Mk 1:21b-28

MP Pss: 5-6	Lessons: Am 1 ♦ Mt 9:18-34
EP 10-11	Am 2 ♦ Gal 2

10 Wed Feria *Green*
DWM 198
Lec 307: 1 Sm 3:1-10, 19-20 ♦ Mk 1:29-39

MP Pss: 119:I-III	Lessons: Am 3 ♦ Mt 9:35-10:23
EP 12-14	Am 4 ♦ Gal 3

11 Thu Feria *Green*
DWM 198
Lec 308: 1 Sm 4:1-11 ♦ Mk 1:40-45

MP Pss: 18:I	Lessons: Am 5 ♦ Mt 10:24-end
EP 18:II	Am 6 ♦ Gal 4:1-5:1

12 Fri Feria *Green*
Or:
St Benedict Biscop, Abbot *White*
Can: *St Marguerite Bourgeoys, Virgin* *White*
DWM 198
Lec 309: 1 Sm 8:4-7, 10-22a ♦ Mk 2:1-12
  Or, for St Benedict Biscop, Abbot: DWM 666
  Or, for St Marguerite Bourgeoys, Virgin: DWM 938

> ❖ Though inscribed in the Canadian National Calendar as an *Obligatory Memorial*, the liturgical observance of St Marguerite Bourgeoys is here listed as an *Optional Memorial*, in deference to the Ordinariate's Particular Calendar and to permit the celebration of St Benedict Biscop.

MP Pss: 16-17   Lessons: Am 7 ♦ Mt 11
EP   22   Am 8 ♦ Gal 5:2-end

13 Sat   Feria   Green
              Or:
              St Hilary, Bishop and Doctor of the Church   *White*
              BVM: Mass of Saint Mary 2   *White*
DWM 198
Lec 310: 1 Sm 9:1-4, 17-19; 10:1a ♦ Mk 2:13-17
      Or, for St Hilary, Bishop and Doctor of the Church: DWM 667
Lec 512: 1 Jn 2:18-25 ♦ Mt 5:13-19 (#730.1)
      Or, for Saint Mary: DWM 991
Lec 707-712 any readings from the Common of the BVM

MP Pss: 20-21   Lessons: Am 9 ♦ Mt 12:1-21
EP 1 of The Second Sunday after Epiphany
      Pss: 110, 116-117   Lessons: Ob ♦ Gal 6

14 SUN   SECOND SUNDAY AFTER THE EPIPHANY (OT 2)   Green
DWM 204 Gloria, Creed
Lec 65: 1 Sm 3:3b-10, 19 ♦ Ps 40:1,3,8-11 ♦ 1 Cor 6:13c-15a, 17-20 ♦ Jn 1:35-42

> ¶ The appointed readings for Year B are cited above, and appear in the RSV-2CE lectionary beginning on page 456. The readings on pp. 453-455 in the RSV-2CE lectionary are those for Year C only and are not options for Year B in the current Roman Lectionary. Sacristans and Readers should consult with the Celebrant or Homilist to ascertain the desired reading before setting the book and before reading.

MP Pss: 148-150   Lessons: Am 3 ♦ Jn 6:22-40   Te Deum
EP 2   114-115   Mi 3:5-end ♦ Jn 4:43-5:9

15 Mon   Feria   Green
DWM 204
Lec 311: 1 Sm 15:16-23 ♦ Mk 2:18-22

MP Pss: 25   Lessons: Jon 1 & 2 ♦ Mt 12:22-end
EP   9, 15   Jon 3 & 4 ♦ 1 Cor 1:1-25

16 Tue   Feria   Green

DWM 204

Lec 312: 1 Sm 16:1-13 ♦ Mk 2:23-28

MP	Pss: 26, 28	Lessons:	Mi 1 ♦ Mt 13:1-23
EP	36, 39		Mi 2 ♦ 1 Cor 1:26-2:end

17 Wed   Saint Anthony, Abbot *Memorial*   White

DWM 667

Lec 313: 1 Sm 17:32-33, 37, 40-51 ♦ Mk 3:1-6

    Or:

Lec 513: Eph 6:10-13, 18 (#740.8) ♦ Mt 19:16-26

MP	Pss: 38	Lessons:	Mi 3 ♦ Mt 13:24-43
EP	119:IV-VI		Mi 4:1-5:1 ♦ 1 Cor 3

18 Thu   Feria   Green

DWM 204

Lec 314: 1 Sm 18:6-9; 19:1-7 ♦ Mk 3:7-12

> ❖ The Week of Prayer for Christian Unity runs from 18 January to 25 January (Conversion of St Paul). On any of these days unimpeded by a Sunday or Memorial, a Mass for Christian Unity (DWM 1008) may be said.

MP	Pss: 37:I	Lessons:	Mi 5:2-end ♦ Mt 13:44-end
EP	37:II		Mi 6 ♦ 1 Cor 4:1-17

19 Fri   Feria   Green

DWM 204

Lec 315: 1 Sm 24:2-20 ♦ Mk 3:13-19

MP	Pss: 31	Lessons:	Mi 7 ♦ Mt 14
EP	35		Na 1 ♦ 1 Cor 4:18-5:end

20 Sat   Feria   Green

              Or:

              St Fabian, Pope and Martyr   *Red*

              St Sebastian, Martyr   *Red*

              BVM: Mass of Saint Mary 2   *White*

DWM 204

Lec 316: 2 Sm 1:1-4, 11-12, 19, 23-27 ♦ Mk 3:20-21

    Or, for St Fabian, Pope and Martyr: DWM 668

Lec 514: 1 Pt 5:1-4 (#722.13) ♦ Jn 21:15-17 (#724.12)

    Or, for St Sebastian, Martyr: DWM 669

Lec 515: 1 Pt 3:14-17 (#716.8) ♦ Mt 10:28-33 (#718.2)
> *Or, for Saint Mary:* DWM 991

Lec 707-712 any readings from the Common of the BVM

MP Pss: 30, 32   Lessons: Na 2 ♦ Mt 15:1-28
EP 1 of The Third Sunday after Epiphany
    Pss: 42-43   Lessons: Na 3 ♦ 1 Cor 6

21 SUN   THIRD SUNDAY AFTER THE EPIPHANY (OT 3)   Green
Sunday of the Word of God
DWM 206 Gloria, Creed
Lec 68: Jon 3:1-5, 10 ♦ Ps 25:3-8 ♦ 1 Cor 7:29-31 ♦ Mk 1:14-20

MP Pss: 63, 98   Lessons: Am 5:6-24 ♦ Jn 6:41-end   Te Deum
EP 2   103   Mi 4:1-7 ♦ Jn 9

22 Mon   USA: Day of Prayer for the Legal Protection of Unborn Children   Green / Mass: Violet or White
Can: Feria   Green
Or:
Can: *St Vincent, Deacon and Martyr*   Red
DWM (USA:) 671 (Can:) 206
USA: Lec: for the Day of Prayer, any of the following readings: Gn 1:1—2:2 (no. 41) *or* 2 Mc 7:1, 20-31 (no. 499) *or* Is 49:1-6 (no. 587) *or* Rom 11:33-36 (no. 121) *or* Eph 1:3-14 (no. 104) *or* Eph 3:14-21 (no. 476) *or* Col 1:12-20 (no. 162) *or* 1 Jn 3:11-21 (no. 208) ♦ Mt 18:1-5, 10, 12-14 (no. 414) *or* Mk 9:30-37 (no. 134) *or* Lk 1:39-56 (no. 622) *or* Lk 17:11-19 (no. 144) *or* Lk 23:35-43 (no. 162) *or* Jn 1:1-5, 9-14, 16-18 (no. 755) *or* Jn 6:24-35 (no. 113); *or* For Peace & Justice (nos. 887-891)
Can: Lec 317: 2 Sm 5:1-7, 10 ♦ Mk 3:22-30
> *Or, for St Vincent, Deacon and Martyr:* DWM 670

Lec 517: 2 Cor 4:7-15 (#716.3) ♦ Mt 10:17-22 (#718.1)

MP Pss: 41, 52   Lessons: Hb 1 ♦ 1 Cor 7
EP   44   Hb 2 ♦ 1 Cor 8

23 Tue   Feria   Green
Or:
USA: *St Vincent, Deacon and Martyr*   Red
USA: *St Marianne Cope, Virgin*   White
DWM 206
Lec 318: 2 Sm 6:12b-15, 17-19 ♦ Mk 3:31-35
> *Or, for St Vincent, Deacon and Martyr:* DWM 670

Lec 517: 2 Cor 4:7-15 (#716.3) ♦ Mt 10:17-22 (#718.1)
> *Or, for St Marianne Cope, Virgin:* DWM 938

January 2024

MP Pss: 45   Lessons: Hb 3:2-end ♦ 1 Cor 9
EP   47-48   Zep 1 ♦ 1 Cor 10-11:1

24 Wed   Saint Francis de Sales, Bishop and Doctor of the Church *Memorial*   White
DWM 672
Lec 319: 2 Sm 7:4-17 ♦ Mk 4:1-20
   Or:
Lec 518: Eph 3:8-12 (#728.4) ♦ Jn 15:9-17 (#742.25)

MP Pss: 119:VII-IX   Lessons: Zep 2 ♦ 1 Cor 11:2-end
EP   49, 53   Zep 3 ♦ 1 Cor 12:1-27

25 Thu   Conversion of Saint Paul the Apostle *Feast*   White
DWM 672 Gloria
Lec 519: Acts 22:3-16 or Acts 9:1-22 ♦ Ps 117:1-2 ♦ Mk 16:15-18

❖ End of the Week of Prayer for Christian Unity.

MP Pss: 19   Lessons: Is 56:1-8 ♦ Gal 1:11-end   Te Deum
EP   119:XII-XIV or   Jer 1:4-10 or Sir 39:1-10 ♦ Phil 3:1-14 or
          96, 98   Acts 26:1-23

26 Fri   Saints Timothy and Titus, Bishops *Memorial*   White
DWM 674
Lec 321: 2 Sm 11:1-4a, 5-10a, 13-17 ♦ Mk 4:26-34
   Or:
Lec 520: **2 Tm 1:1-8 or Ti 1:1-5** ♦ Lk 10:1-9 (#724.8)

MP Pss: 40, 54   Lessons: Mal 1 ♦ 1 Cor 14:20-end
EP   51   Mal 2:1-16 ♦ 1 Cor 15:1-34

27 Sat   Feria   Green
   Or:
   St Angela Merici, Virgin   *White*
   BVM: Mass of Saint Mary 2   *White*
DWM 206
Lec 322: 2 Sm 12:1-7a, 10-17 ♦ Mk 4:35-41
   Or, for St Angela Merici, Virgin: DWM 675
Lec 521: 1 Pt 4:7b-11 (#740.15) ♦ Mk 9:34-37 (#742.15)
   Or, for Saint Mary: DWM 991
Lec 707-712 any readings from the Common of the BVM

MP Pss: 55   Lessons: Mal 2:17-3:12 ♦ 1 Cor 15:35-end
EP 1 of SEPTUAGESIMA
   Pss: 138-139   Lessons: Mal 3:13-4:end ♦ 1 Cor 16

28 SUN   THE SUNDAY CALLED SEPTUAGESIMA OR THIRD SUNDAY BEFORE   Violet
   LENT (OT 4)
DWM 214 Creed
Lec 71: Dt 18:15-20 ♦ Ps 95:1-2, 6-9 ♦ 1 Cor 7:32-35 ♦ Mk 1:21b-28

MP Pss: 118   Lessons: Gn 1:1-2:3 ♦ Rv 21:1-7
EP 2   145   Gn 2:4-end ♦ Mk 10:1-16

29 Mon   Pre-Lenten Feria   Violet
DWM 214
Lec 323: 2 Sm 15:13-14, 30; 16:5-13a ♦ Mk 5:1-20

MP Pss: 106:I   Lessons: Gn 3 ♦ Mt 15:29-16:12
EP   106:II   Gn 4:1-16 ♦ Rom 1

30 Tue   Pre-Lenten Feria   Violet
DWM 214
Lec 324: 2 Sm 18:9-10, 14b, 24-25a, 30-19:3 ♦ Mk 5:21-43

MP Pss: 120-123   Lessons: Gn 6:5-end ♦ Mt 16:13-end
EP   124-127   Gn 7 ♦ Rom 2

31 Wed   Saint John Bosco, Priest *Memorial*   White
DWM 677
Lec 325: 2 Sm 24:2, 9-17 ♦ Mk 6:1-6
  Or:
Lec 523: Phil 4:4-9 (#740.10) ♦ Mt 18:1-5 (#742.7)

MP Pss: 119:XIX-XXII   Lessons: Gn 8:1-14 ♦ Mt 17:1-23
EP   128-130   Gn 8:15-9:17 ♦ Rom 3

February 2024

1 Thu Pre-Lenten Feria Violet
DWM 214
Lec 326: 1 Kgs 2:1-4, 10-12 ♦ Mk 6:7-13

MP	Pss: 131-133	Lessons:	Gn 11:1-9 ♦ Mt 17:24-18:14
EP	134-135		Gn 11:27-12:10 ♦ Rom 4

2 Fri Presentation of the Lord *Feast* White
DWM 679 Gloria
Lec 524: Mal 3:1-4 ♦ Ps 24:7-10 ♦ Heb 2:14-18 ♦ Lk 2:22-40 or 2:22-32

> ¶ The Blessing of Candles with the Procession or Solemn Entrance may occur at Mass on this day (DWM 679-682).
>
> ❖ Anniversary of the Episcopal Ordination of the Most Rev. Steven J. Lopes, first Bishop of the Personal Ordinariate of the Chair of Saint Peter.

MP	Pss: 42-43	Lessons:	1 Sm 1:21-end ♦ Heb 10:1-10	Te Deum
EP	48, 87		Hg 2:1-9 ♦ Rom 12:1-5	

3 Sat Pre-Lenten Feria Violet
Or:
St Blaise, Bishop and Martyr *Red*
St Ansgar, Bishop *White*
BVM: Mass of Saint Mary 3 *White*
DWM 214
Lec 328: 1 Kgs 3:4-13 ♦ Mk 6:30-34
  Or, for St Blaise, Bishop and Martyr: DWM 684
Lec 525: Rom 5:1-5 (#716.1) ♦ Mk 16:15-20 (#724.6)
  Or, for St Ansgar, Bishop: DWM 685
Lec 526: Is 52:7-10 (#719.5) ♦ Mk 1:14-20 (#724.5)
  Or, for Saint Mary: DWM 993
Lec 707-712 any readings from the Common of the BVM

MP	Pss: 137, 144	Lessons:	Gn 15 ♦ Mt 19:1-15
EP 1 of SEXAGESIMA			
	Pss: 104	Lessons:	Gn 16 ♦ Rom 6

> ¶ *Ave Regina Caelorum* may be said after EP or Compline after Candlemas (i.e. beginning 3 Feb) to Wednesday in Holy Week.

4 SUN   THE SUNDAY CALLED SEXAGESIMA OR SECOND SUNDAY BEFORE   Violet
         LENT (OT 5)

DWM 216 Creed

Lec 74: Jb 7:1-4, 6-7 ♦ Ps 147:1-6 ♦ 1 Cor 9:16-19, 22-23 ♦ Mk 1:29-39

MP Pss: 146-147	Lessons: Gn 3 ♦ 1 Cor 6:12-end	
EP 2 111-113	Gn 37 ♦ Lk 10:25-37	

5 Mon   Saint Agatha, Virgin and Martyr *Memorial*   Red

DWM 685

Lec 329: 1 Kgs 8:1-7, 9-13 ♦ Mk 6:53-56
     Or:
Lec 527: 1 Cor 1:26-31 (#740.2) ♦ Lk 9:23-26 (#718.4)

MP Pss: 1-3	Lessons: Gn 17:1-22 ♦ Mt 19:16-20:16	
EP 4, 7	Gn 18 ♦ Rom 7	

6 Tue   Saint Paul Miki and Companions, Martyrs *Memorial*   Red

DWM 687

Lec 330: 1 Kgs 8:22-23, 27-30 ♦ Mk 7:1-13
     Or:
Lec 528: Gal 2:19-20 (#740.5) ♦ Mt 28:16-20

MP Pss: 5-6	Lessons: Gn 19:1-3,12-29 ♦ Mt 20:17-end	
EP 10-11	Gn 21 ♦ Rom 8:1-17	

7 Wed   Pre-Lenten Feria   Violet

DWM 216

Lec 331: 1 Kgs 10:1-10 ♦ Mk 7:14-23

MP Pss: 119:I-III	Lessons: Gn 22:1-19 ♦ Mt 21:1-22	
EP 12-14	Gn 23 ♦ Rom 8:18-end	

8 Thu   Pre-Lenten Feria   Violet
     Or:
     St Jerome Emiliani, Priest   *White*
     St Josephine Bakhita, Virgin   *White*

DWM 216

Lec 332: 1 Kgs 11:4-13 ♦ Mk 7:24-30
     Or, for St Jerome Emiliani, Priest: DWM 688
Lec 529: Tb 12:6-13 (#737.8) ♦ Mk 10:17-30 or 10:17-27 (#742.17)
     Or, for St Josephine Bakhita, Virgin: DWM 689

February 2024

MP Pss: 18:I   Lessons: Gn 24:1-28 ♦ Mt 21:23-end
EP   18:II   Gn 24:29-end ♦ Rom 9

9 Fri Pre-Lenten Feria   Violet
DWM 216
Lec 333: 1 Kgs 11:29-32; 12:19 ♦ Mk 7:31-37

MP Pss: 16-17   Lessons: Gn 25:7-11,19-end ♦ Mt 22:1-33
EP   22   Gn 27:1-40 ♦ Rom 10

10 Sat Saint Scholastica, Virgin *Memorial*   White
DWM 690
Lec 334: 1 Kgs 12:26-32; 13:33-34 ♦ Mk 8:1-10
    Or:
Lec 530: Sg 8:6-7 (#731.1) ♦ Lk 10:38-42 (#736.3)

MP Pss: 20-21   Lessons: Gn 27:41-28:end ♦ Mt 22:34-23:12
EP 1 of QUINQUAGESIMA
    Pss: 110, 116-117   Lessons: Gn 29:1-20 ♦ Rom 11

11 SUN THE SUNDAY CALLED QUINQUAGESIMA OR SUNDAY NEXT   Violet
    BEFORE LENT (OT 6)
DWM 218 Creed
Lec 77: Lv 13:1-2, 44-46 ♦ Ps 32:1-2, 5-6, 8, 12 ♦ 1 Cor 10:31-11:1 ♦ Mk 1:40-45

MP Pss: 148-150   Lessons: Gn 12:1-9 ♦ 1 Cor 12:4-end
EP 2   114-115   Gn 41:1-40 ♦ 1 Jn 4:7-end

12 Mon Pre-Lenten Feria   Violet
DWM 218
Lec 335: Jas 1:1-11 ♦ Mk 8:11-13

MP Pss: 25   Lessons: Gn 31:1-9,14-21 ♦ Mt 23:13-end
EP   9, 15   Gn 31:22-32:2 ♦ Rom 12

13 Tue Pre-Lenten Feria (Shrove Tuesday)   Violet
DWM 218
Lec 336: Jas 1:12-18 ♦ Mk 8:14-21

MP Pss: 26, 28   Lessons: Gn 32:3-30 ♦ Mt 24:1-28
EP   36, 39   Gn 33 ♦ Rom 13

> ❖ However, at the Cathedral, it is the Eve of the Solemnity of the Anniversary of the Dedication of the Cathedral of our Lady of Walsingham.
> EP 1 of the Solemnity of the Anniversary is observed
> Pss: 48, 122 Lessons: Hag 2:1-9 ♦ 1 Cor 3:9-17

14 Wed   Ash Wednesday   Violet

DWM 223

Lec 219: Jl 2:12-18 ♦ 2 Cor 5:20-6:2 ♦ Ps 51:1-4, 10-11, 12, 15 ♦ Mt 6:1-6, 16-18

> ¶ The Penitential Office for the Blessing and Imposition of Ashes may be used before Mass (DWM 223), or ashes may be blessed and distributed during Mass (DWM 228).
>
> ¶ The Lent Prose may be sung during the distribution of Ashes (DWM 222).
>
> ¶ Note that DWM prescribes a genuflection at the Tract *Domine, non secundum* on Ash Wednesday and whenever else it occurs (on Mondays, Wednesdays, and Fridays during Lent): "... for we are come to great misery. [*Here genuflect*] V. Help us, O God ..." (DWM 230).
>
> ¶ "Optional Prayers over the People are provided for the Sundays and weekdays of Lent. These prayers, which have a penitential character, implore a special gift of grace for perseverance in Lenten discipline, so as to reap their spiritual fruits. Following the Postcommunion prayer, the Priest introduces the Prayer over the People with the invitation *The Lord be with you.* The Deacon or, if necessary, the Priest himself then says *Bow down before the Lord* followed by the Prayer over the People. The Priest proceeds immediately to the blessing, omitting in this case *The peace of God...* and saying only ... *and the blessing of God Almighty* while imparting the blessing" (DWM 129, 231).

MP   Pss: 32, 143   Lessons: Is 58 ♦ Mk 2:13-22

EP   102, 130   Dn 9:3-19 ♦ Heb 3:12-4:13

15 Thu   Thursday After Ash Wednesday   Violet

DWM 232

Lec 220: Dt 30:15-20 ♦ Lk 9:22-25

MP   Pss: 37:I   Lessons: Gn 35:1-20 ♦ Mt 24:29-end

EP   37:II   Gn 37 ♦ Rom 14

16 Fri   Friday After Ash Wednesday   Violet

DWM 234

Lec 221: Is 58:1-9a ♦ Mt 9:14-15

MP   Pss: 31   Lessons: Gn 39 ♦ Mt 25:1-30

EP   35   Gn 40 ♦ Rom 15

17 Sat   Saturday After Ash Wednesday   Violet

[The Seven Holy Founders of the Servite Order]

BVM: Mass of Saint Mary 3

DWM 236

Lec 222: Is 58:9c-14 ♦ Lk 5:27-32

> *Or, for The Seven Holy Founders of the Servite Order:* DWM 693 – if commemorated, Collect only
>
> *Or, for Saint Mary:* DWM 993

Lec 707-712 any readings from the Common of the BVM

MP Pss: 30, 32   Lessons: Gn 41:1-40 ♦ Mt 25:31-end

EP 1 of The First Sunday in Lent

       Pss: 42-43   Lessons: Gn 41:41-end ♦ Rom 16

18 SUN   FIRST SUNDAY IN LENT   Violet

DWM 238 Creed

Lec 23: Gn 9:8-15 ♦ Ps 25:3-8 ♦ 1 Pt 3:18-22 ♦ Mk 1:12-15

> ¶ The Litany may be sung in procession before the principal Sunday Mass (DWM 1061).
>
> ¶ The Lent Prose may be sung on any of the Sundays in Lent (DWM 222).
>
> ¶ Where it is the custom, on any of the Sundays in Lent, when the Litany does not precede Mass, the Decalogue may be sung or said (replacing the Summary of the Law and the Kyrie) (DWM 1046).

MP Pss: 63, 98   Lessons: Gn 27:1-40 ♦ Heb 4:14-5:10

EP 2   103   Gn 42 ♦ Lk 22:1-23

19 Mon   Monday in the First Week of Lent   Violet

DWM 240

Lec 224: Lv 19:1-2, 11-18 ♦ Mt 25:31-46

MP Pss: 41, 52   Lessons: Gn 43:1-14 ♦ Mt 26:1-30

EP   44   Gn 43:15-end ♦ Phil 1

20 Tue   Tuesday in the First Week of Lent   Violet

DWM 242

Lec 225: Is 55:10-11 ♦ Mt 6:7-15

MP Pss: 45   Lessons: Gn 44 ♦ Mt 26:31-56

EP   47-48   Gn 45:1-15 ♦ Phil 2

21 Wed   Ember Wednesday in Lent   Violet

       [*St Peter Damian, Bishop and Doctor of the Church*]

DWM 244

Lec 226: Jon 3:1-10 ♦ Lk 11:29-32

St Peter Damian, Bishop and Doctor of the Church may optionally be commemorated only in the Daily Office by adding the DWM 694 Collect after the Collect of the Day.

MP Pss: 119:VII-IX   Lessons: Gn 45:16-46:7 ♦ Mt 26:57-end
EP 1 of THE CHAIR OF ST PETER
        Pss: 48, 122 or 84, 150 Lessons: Is 43:10-15 ♦ Mt 9:35-10:4

22 Thu   CHAIR OF SAINT PETER THE APOSTLE *Solemnity*   White
DWM 694 Gloria, Creed
Lec 121: Is 22:19-23 ♦ Lec 535: 1 Pt 5:1-4 ♦ Mt 16:13-19

MP Pss: 66-67   Lessons: Ez 3:4-11 ♦ Jn 21:15-22   Te Deum
EP 2   118   Ez 34:11-16 ♦ Acts 11:1-18

23 Fri   Ember Friday in Lent   Violet
        [*St Polycarp, Bishop and Martyr*]
DWM 248
Lec 228: Ez 18:21-28 ♦ Mt 5:20-26
St Polycarp, Bishop and Martyr may optionally be commemorated only in the
Daily Office by adding the DWM 696 Collect after the Collect of the Day.

MP Pss: 40, 54   Lessons: Gn 49:1-32 ♦ Mt 27:27-56
EP   51   Gn 49:33-50:end ♦ Col 1:1-20

24 Sat   Ember Saturday in Lent   Violet
DWM 250
Lec 229: Dt 26:16-19 ♦ Mt 5:43-48

MP Pss: 55   Lessons: Ex 1:1-14, 22-2:10 ♦ Mt 27:57-28:end
EP 1 of The Second Sunday in Lent
        Pss: 138-139   Lessons: Ex 2:11-22 ♦ Col 1:21-2:7

25 SUN   SECOND SUNDAY IN LENT   Violet
DWM 252 Creed
Lec 26: Gn 22:1-2, 9a, 10-13, 15-18 ♦ Ps 116:9-10, 13-16 ♦ Rom 8:31b-34 ♦ Mk 9:2-10

MP Pss: 24, 29   Lessons: Gn 28:10-end ♦ Heb 10:19-end
EP 2   8, 84   Gn 43:1-15(16-26), 27-end ♦ Lk 22:24-53

26 Mon   Monday in the Second Week of Lent   Violet
DWM 254
Lec 230: Dn 9:4b-10 ♦ Lk 6:36-38

MP	Pss: 56-58	Lessons: Ex 2:23-3:end ♦ Jn 1:1-28
EP	64-65	Ex 4:1-23 ♦ Col 2:8-3:11

27 Tue   Tuesday in the Second Week of Lent   Violet

[St Gregory of Narek, Abbot and Doctor of the Church]

DWM 256

Lec 231: Is 1:10, 16-20 ♦ Mt 23:1-12

> *Or, for St Gregory of Narek, Abbot and Doctor of the Church:* DWM 936 – if commemorated, Collect only

MP	Pss: 61-62	Lessons: Ex 4:27-6:1 ♦ Jn 1:29-end
EP	68	Ex 6:2-13, 7:1-7 ♦ Col 3:12-4:1

28 Wed   Wednesday in the Second Week of Lent   Violet

DWM 258

Lec 232: Jer 18:18-20 ♦ Mt 20:17-28

MP	Pss: 72	Lessons: Ex 7:8-end ♦ Jn 2
EP	119:X-XII	Ex 8:1-19 ♦ Col 4:2-end

29 Thu   Thursday in the Second Week of Lent   Violet

DWM 260

Lec 233: Jer 17:5-10 ♦ Lk 16:19-31

MP	Pss: 70-71	Lessons: Ex 8:20-9:12 ♦ Jn 3:1-21
EP	74	Ex 9:13-end ♦ Phlm

March 2024

1 Fri   Friday in the Second Week of Lent   Violet
                [*St David, Bishop*]

DWM 262

Lec 234: Gn 37:3-4, 12-13a, 17b-28 ♦ Mt 21:33-43, 45-46

     Or, for St David, Bishop: DWM 697 – if commemorated, Collect only

MP	Pss: 69	Lessons:	Ex 10:1-20 ♦ Jn 3:22-end
EP	73		Ex 10:21-11:end ♦ Eph 1

2 Sat   Saturday in the Second Week of Lent   Violet
                BVM: Mass of Saint Mary 3

DWM 264

Lec 235: Mi 7:14-15, 18-20 ♦ Lk 15:1-3, 11-32

     Or, for Saint Mary: DWM 993

Lec 707-712 any readings from the Common of the BVM

MP	Pss: 75-76	Lessons:	Ex 12:1-20 ♦ Jn 4:1-26
EP 1 of The Third Sunday in Lent			
	Pss: 23, 27	Lessons:	Ex 12:21-36 ♦ Eph 2

3 SUN   THIRD SUNDAY IN LENT   Violet

DWM 266 Creed

Lec 29: Ex 20:1-17 or 20:1-3, 7-8, 12-17 ♦ Ps 19:7-10 ♦ 1 Cor 1:22-25 ♦ Jn 2:13-25

> ¶ The readings cited above are the appointed readings for the current year in the three-year cycle. The readings for Year A, Lec 28, which are duplicated in the RSV-2CE lectionary and appear before the current year's readings, may be used in place of these, especially when the OCIA Scrutinies are celebrated, in which case the long form of the readings should also be selected. Sacristans and Readers should consult with the Celebrant or Homilist to ascertain the desired reading before setting the book and before reading.

MP	Pss: 93, 96	Lessons:	Gn 29:1-20 ♦ Heb 12:14-end
EP 2	34		Gn 44:1-45:8 ♦ Lk 22:54-end

4 Mon   Monday in the Third Week of Lent   Violet
                [*St Casimir*]

DWM 268

Lec 237: 2 Kgs 5:1-15a ♦ Lk 4:24-30

Or the following Mass which may be used on any day of this week, especially in Years B and C when the Gospel of the Samaritan woman is not read on the Third Sunday of Lent.

Lec 236: Ex 17:1-7 ♦ Jn 4:5-42

Or, for St Casimir: DWM 699 – if commemorated, Collect only

MP	Pss: 80	Lessons:	Ex 12:37-end ♦ Jn 4:27-end
EP	77, 79		Ex 13:1-16 ♦ Eph 3

5 Tue   Tuesday in the Third Week of Lent   Violet

DWM 270

Lec 238: Dn 3:*Song of the Three Children 2, 11-20* ♦ Mt 18:21-35

Or the following Mass which may be used on any day of this week, especially in Years B and C when the Gospel of the Samaritan woman is not read on the Third Sunday of Lent.

Lec 236: Ex 17:1-7 ♦ Jn 4:5-42

MP	Pss: 78:I	Lessons:	Ex 13:17-14:14 ♦ Jn 5:1-23
EP	78:II		Ex 14:15-end ♦ Eph 4:1-16

6 Wed   Wednesday in the Third Week of Lent   Violet

DWM 272

Lec 239: Dt 4:1, 5-9 ♦ Mt 5:17-19

Or the following Mass which may be used on any day of this week, especially in Years B and C when the Gospel of the Samaritan woman is not read on the Third Sunday of Lent.

Lec 236: Ex 17:1-7 ♦ Jn 4:5-42

MP	Pss: 119:XIII-XV	Lessons:	Ex 15:1-26 ♦ Jn 5:24-end
EP	81-82		Ex 15:27-16:35 ♦ Eph 4:17-30

7 Thu   Thursday in the Third Week of Lent   Violet
            [*Sts Perpetua and Felicitas, Martyrs*]

DWM 274

Lec 240: Jer 7:23-28 ♦ Lk 11:14-23

Or the following Mass which may be used on any day of this week, especially in Years B and C when the Gospel of the Samaritan woman is not read on the Third Sunday of Lent.

Lec 236: Ex 17:1-7 ♦ Jn 4:5-42

Or, for Sts Perpetua and Felicitas, Martyrs: DWM 699 – if commemorated, Collect only

MP	Pss: 83	Lessons:	Ex 17 ♦ Jn 6:1-21
EP	85-86		Ex 18 ♦ Eph 4:31-5:21

March 2024

8 Fri   Friday in the Third Week of Lent   Violet
[St John of God, Religious]

DWM 276

Lec 241: Hos 14:1-9 ♦ Mk 12:28b-34

Or the following Mass which may be used on any day of this week, especially in Years B and C when the Gospel of the Samaritan woman is not read on the Third Sunday of Lent.

Lec 236: Ex 17:1-7 ♦ Jn 4:5-42

Or, for St John of God, Religious: DWM 701 – if commemorated, Collect only

MP Pss: 88	Lessons:	Ex 19 ♦ Jn 6:22-40
EP 91-92		Ex 20:1-21 ♦ Eph 5:22-6:9

9 Sat   Saturday in the Third Week of Lent   Violet
[St Frances of Rome, Religious]
BVM: Mass of Saint Mary 3

DWM 278

Lec 242: Hos 6:1-6 ♦ Lk 18:9-14

Or the following Mass which may be used on any day of this week, especially in Years B and C when the Gospel of the Samaritan woman is not read on the Third Sunday of Lent.

Lec 236: Ex 17:1-7 ♦ Jn 4:5-42

Or, for St Frances of Rome, Religious: DWM 701 – if commemorated, Collect only

Or, for Saint Mary: DWM 993

Lec 707-712 any readings from the Common of the BVM

MP Pss: 87, 90	Lessons:	Ex 22:20-23:17 ♦ Jn 6:41-end

EP 1 of The Fourth Sunday in Lent

Pss: 136	Lessons:	Ex 23:20-end ♦ Eph 6:10-end

10 SUN   FOURTH SUNDAY IN LENT   Rose/Violet

DWM 280 Creed

Lec 32: 2 Chr 36:14-16, 19-23 ♦ Ps 137:1-6 ♦ Eph 2:4-10 ♦ Jn 3:14-21

> ¶ The readings cited above are the appointed readings for the current year in the three-year cycle. The readings for Year A, Lec 31, which are duplicated in the RSV-2CE lectionary and appear before the current year's readings, may be used in place of these, especially when the OCIA Scrutinies are celebrated, in which case the long form of the readings should also be selected. Sacristans and Readers should consult with the Celebrant or Homilist to ascertain the desired reading before setting the book and before reading.

MP Pss: 66-67	Lessons:	Gn 32:3-30 ♦ Heb 13:1-21
EP 2 19, 46		Gn 45:16-46:7 ♦ Lk 23:1-25

11 Mon	Monday in the Fourth Week of Lent		Violet

DWM 282

Lec 244: Is 65:17-21 ♦ Jn 4:43-54

Or the following Mass which may be used on any day of this week, especially in Years B and C when the Gospel of the man born blind is not read on the Fourth Sunday of Lent.

Lec 243: Mi 7:7-9 ♦ Jn 9:1-41

MP	Pss: 89:I	Lessons: Ex 24 ♦ Jn 7:1-24	
EP	89:II	Ex 25:1-22 ♦ 1 Tm 1:1-17	

12 Tue	Tuesday in the Fourth Week of Lent		Violet

DWM 284

Lec 245: Ez 47:1-9, 12 ♦ Jn 5:1-3a, 5-16

Or the following Mass which may be used on any day of this week, especially in Years B and C when the Gospel of the man born blind is not read on the Fourth Sunday of Lent.

Lec 243: Mi 7:7-9 ♦ Jn 9:1-41

MP	Pss: 97, 99-100	Lessons: Ex 28:1-4, 29:1-9 ♦ Jn 7:25-end	
EP	94-(95)	Ex 29:38-30:16 ♦ 1 Tm 1:18-2:end	

13 Wed	Wednesday in the Fourth Week of Lent		Violet

DWM 286

Lec 246: Is 49:8-15 ♦ Jn 5:17-30

Or the following Mass which may be used on any day of this week, especially in Years B and C when the Gospel of the man born blind is not read on the Fourth Sunday of Lent.

Lec 243: Mi 7:7-9 ♦ Jn 9:1-41

MP	Pss: 101, 109	Lessons: Ex 32 ♦ Jn 8:1-30	
EP	119:XVI-XVIII	Ex 33 ♦ 1 Tm 3	

14 Thu	Thursday in the Fourth Week of Lent		Violet

DWM 288

Lec 247: Ex 32:7-14 ♦ Jn 5:31-47

Or the following Mass which may be used on any day of this week, especially in Years B and C when the Gospel of the man born blind is not read on the Fourth Sunday of Lent.

Lec 243: Mi 7:7-9 ♦ Jn 9:1-41

MP	Pss: 69	Lessons: Ex 34 ♦ Jn 8:31-end	
EP	73	Ex 35:20-36:7 ♦ 1 Tm 4	

15 Fri   Friday in the Fourth Week of Lent   Violet
          DWM 290
          Lec 248: Wis 2:1a, 12-22 ♦ Jn 7:1-2, 10, 25-30
          Or the following Mass which may be used on any day of this week, especially
          in Years B and C when the Gospel of the man born blind is not read on the
          Fourth Sunday of Lent.
          Lec 243: Mi 7:7-9 ♦ Jn 9:1-41

          MP Pss: 102   Lessons: Ex 40:17-end ♦ Jn 9
          EP   107:I   Lv 6:8-end ♦ 1 Tm 5

16 Sat   Saturday in the Fourth Week of Lent   Violet
                 BVM: Mass of Saint Mary 3
          DWM 292
          Lec 249: Jer 11:18-20 ♦ Jn 7:40-53
          Or the following Mass which may be used on any day of this week, especially
          in Years B and C when the Gospel of the man born blind is not read on the
          Fourth Sunday of Lent.
          Lec 243: Mi 7:7-9 ♦ Jn 9:1-41
                 Or, for Saint Mary: DWM 993
          Lec 707-712 any readings from the Common of the BVM

          MP Pss: 107:II, 108   Lessons: Lv 19:1-18, 30-end ♦ Jn 10:1-21
          EP 1 of The Fifth Sunday in Lent
                 Pss: 33   Lessons: Lv 25:1-24 ♦ 1 Tm 6

17 SUN   FIFTH SUNDAY IN LENT COMMONLY CALLED PASSION SUNDAY   Violet
          DWM 294 Creed
          Lec 35: Jer 31:31-34 ♦ Ps 51:1-2, 10-13 ♦ Heb 5:7-9 ♦ Jn 12:20-33

> ¶ The readings cited above are the appointed readings for the current year in the three-year cycle. The readings for Year A, Lec 34, which are duplicated in the RSV-2CE lectionary and appear before the current year's readings, may be used in place of these, especially when the OCIA Scrutinies are celebrated, in which case the long form of the readings should also be selected. Sacristans and Readers should consult with the Celebrant or Homilist to ascertain the desired reading before setting the book and before reading.
>
> ¶ "The practice of covering crosses and images throughout the church from this Sunday until the Easter Vigil may be observed" (DWM 294).
>
> ¶ "From the Fifth Sunday in Lent until Maundy Thursday, Psalm 43 is omitted from the Prayers of Preparation, and the Glory be is not said at the *Asperges,* Introit, and the *Lavabo* psalm, except on a feast day, if any shall occur" (DWM 294).
>
> ¶ The Litany may be sung in procession before the principal Sunday Mass (DWM 1061).

MP Pss: 118	Lessons: Ex 2:23-3:20 ♦ Mt 20:17-28	
EP 2 145	Ex 6:2-13 ♦ Lk 23:26-49	

18 Mon   Monday in Passion Week   Violet

[*St Cyril of Jerusalem, Bishop and Doctor of the Church*]

DWM 296

Lec 251: Dn 13:1-9, 15-17, 19-30, 33-62 or 13:41c-62 ♦ Jn 8:1-11

Or the following Mass which may be used on any day of this week, especially in Years B and C when the Gospel of Lazarus is not read on the Fifth Sunday of Lent.

Lec 250: 2 Kgs 4:18b-21, 32-37 ♦ Jn 11:1-45

Or, for St Cyril of Jerusalem, Bishop and Doctor of the Church: DWM 703 – if commemorated, Collect only

MP Pss: 31	Lessons: Nm 6 ♦ Jn 10:22-end	
EP 1 of ST JOSEPH		
Pss: 110-112	Lessons: Hos 11:1-9 ♦ Lk 2:41-52	

19 Tue   SAINT JOSEPH, SPOUSE OF THE BLESSED VIRGIN MARY *Solemnity*   White

DWM 704 Gloria, Creed

Lec 543: 2 Sm 7:4-5a, 12-14a, 16 ♦ Ps 89:1-4, 27, 29 ♦ Rom 4:13, 16-18, 22 ♦ Mt 1:16, 18-21, 24a or Lk 2:41-51a

> † The Rev. Lucien Lindsey, Jr., March 19, 2018

MP Pss: 132	Lessons: Is 11:1-10 ♦ Mt 13:54-58 Te Deum	
EP 2 34	Gn 50:22-26 ♦ Mt 2:12-23	

20 Wed   Wednesday in Passion Week   Violet

DWM 300

Lec 253: Dn 3:14-20, 24-25, 28 RSV-2CE ♦ Jn 8:31-42

Or the following Mass which may be used on any day of this week, especially in Years B and C when the Gospel of Lazarus is not read on the Fifth Sunday of Lent.

Lec 250: 2 Kgs 4:18b-21, 32-37 ♦ Jn 11:1-45

MP Pss: 119:XIX-XXII	Lessons: Nm 13:1-3,17-end ♦ Jn 11:45-end	
EP 128-130	Nm 14:1-25 ♦ 2 Tm 1	

21 Thu   Thursday in Passion Week   Violet

DWM 302

Lec 254: Gn 17:3-9 ♦ Jn 8:51-59

Or the following Mass which may be used on any day of this week, especially in Years B and C when the Gospel of Lazarus is not read on the Fifth Sunday of Lent.

Lec 250: 2 Kgs 4:18b-21, 32-37 ♦ Jn 11:1-45

> Chrism Mass
> DWM 334 Gloria
> Lec 260: Is 61:1-3abcd, 6a, 8b-9 ♦ Rev 1:5-8 ♦ Lk 4:16-21
> ❖ The Bishop will celebrate the Ordinariate's Chrism Mass on Thursday in Passion Week at the Cathedral of Our Lady of Walsingham.

MP Pss: 131-133   Lessons: Nm 16:1-35 ♦ Jn 12:1-19
EP   140, 142   Nm 16:36-17:end ♦ 2 Tm 2

22 Fri   Saint Mary in Passiontide: Friday in Passion Week   Violet

DWM 304

Lec 255: Jer 20:10-13 ♦ Jn 10:31-42

Or the following Mass which may be used on any day of this week, especially in Years B and C when the Gospel of Lazarus is not read on the Fifth Sunday of Lent.

Lec 250: 2 Kgs 4:18b-21, 32-37 ♦ Jn 11:1-45

> ¶ "The Sequence *Stabat Mater* may be sung or said" after the Tract (DWM 305).

MP Pss: 22   Lessons: Nm 20 ♦ Jn 12:20-end
EP   141, 143   Nm 22:1-35 ♦ 2 Tm 3

23 Sat   Saturday in Passion Week   Violet

[*St Turibius de Mogrovejo, Bishop*]

DWM 308

Lec 256: Ez 37:21-28 ♦ Jn 11:45-57

Or the following Mass which may be used on any day of this week, especially in Years B and C when the Gospel of Lazarus is not read on the Fifth Sunday of Lent.

Lec 250: 2 Kgs 4:18b-21, 32-37 ♦ Jn 11:1-45

Or, for St Turibius de Mogrovejo, Bishop: DWM 705 – if commemorated, Collect only

MP Pss: 137, 144   Lessons: Nm 22:36-23:26 ♦ Jn 13
EP 1 of PALM SUNDAY
        Pss: 42-43   Lessons: Nm 23:27-24:end ♦ 2 Tm 4

24 SUN   PALM SUNDAY: THE SECOND SUNDAY IN PASSIONTIDE   Red

DWM 313 (Procession), 325 (Mass) Creed

Lec 37: Mk 11:1-10 or Jn 12:12-16 (The Palm Gospel at the Procession)

Lec 38: Is 50:4-7 ♦ Ps 22:1, 7-8, 16-19, 22-23 ♦ Phil 2:6-11 ♦ Mk 14:1-15:47 or 15:1-39

March 2024

> ¶ "On this day the Church recalls the entrance of Christ the Lord into Jerusalem to accomplish his Paschal Mystery. Accordingly, the commemoration of this entrance of the Lord takes place at all Masses, by means of the Procession before the principal Mass or the Solemn Entrance. The Solemn Entrance, but not the Procession, may be repeated before other Masses" (DWM 313).

MP Pss: 24, 29   Lessons: Ex 11 ♦ Mt 26
EP 2   103   Is 52:13-53:end ♦ Lk 19:29-end

25 Mon   Monday in Holy Week   Violet
DWM 328
Lec 257: Is 42:1-7 ♦ Jn 12:1-11

MP Pss: 51   Lessons: Lam 1:1-12 ♦ Jn 14:1-14
EP   69:1-22   Lam 2:8-19 ♦ Jn 14:15-end

26 Tue   Tuesday in Holy Week   Violet
DWM 330
Lec 258: Is 49:1-6 ♦ Jn 13:21-33, 36-38

MP Pss: 6, 12   Lessons: Lam 3:1-30 ♦ Jn 15:1-16
EP   94   Lam 3:40-51 ♦ Jn 15:17-end

27 Wed   Wednesday in Holy Week   Violet
DWM 332
Lec 259: Is 50:4-9a ♦ Mt 26:14-25

MP Pss: 55   Lessons: Is 42:1-9 ♦ Jn 16:1-15
EP   74   Nm 21:4-9 ♦ Jn 16:16-end

28 Thu   Thursday in Holy Week Commonly Called Maundy Thursday   Violet/White
Mass of the Lord's Supper
DWM 343 Gloria
Lec 39: Ex 12:1-8, 11-14 ♦ Ps 116:11-16 ♦ 1 Cor 11:23-26 ♦ Jn 13:1-15

> ¶ "After the homily there may follow the ceremony of the Maundy. Twelve seats are prepared in a suitable place for the twelve men whose feet are to be washed. The servers lead the men who have been chosen to the place prepared. Then the Priest, removing his chasuble if necessary, goes to each one and, with the help of the Deacon and servers, pours water over each one's feet and then dries them" (DWM 344).
>
> ¶ DWM propers for the Mass of the Lord's Supper include the complete text of the Roman Canon with the proper formulas for the *Communicantes, Hanc igitur* and *Qui pridie* provided (DWM 348).
>
> ¶ After the Postcommunion, the Solemn Translation and Reservation of the Blessed Sacrament follows (DWM 353), after which the rites of Maundy Thursday may conclude with the Rite for the Stripping of the Altars and adoration before the Blessed Sacrament during the night at the Altar of Repose (DWM 354).

MP Pss: 102   Lessons: Ex 24:1-11 ♦ Jn 17
EP   142-143   Lv 16:2-24 ♦ Jn 13:1-35

> ¶ "Evening Prayer is not celebrated by those who have attended the Mass of the Lord's Supper" (DWM 354).

29 Fri   Good Friday: the Passion and Death of Our Lord   Black / Red
DWM 357

Lec 40: Is 52:13-53:12 ♦ Ps 31:1, 6, 13-14, 16-18, 27 ♦ Heb 4:14-16; 5:7-9 ♦ Jn 18:1-19:42

> ¶ "On this and the following day, by most ancient tradition, the Church does not celebrate the Sacraments at all, except for Penance and Anointing of the Sick. The altar should be completely bare, without a cross, without candles and without cloths. The celebration of the Passion and Death of Our Lord takes place on the afternoon of this day, unless a later hour is chosen for a pastoral reason. The celebration consists of three parts: the Liturgy of the Word, the Adoration of the Cross, and Holy Communion" (DWM 357).

MP Pss: 22   Lessons: Gn 22:1-18 ♦ Heb 10:1-10
EP   40, 54   Is 50:4-10 ♦ 1 Pt 2:11-20

> ¶ "Evening Prayer is not celebrated by those who have been present at the solemn liturgical celebration of the Passion of Our Lord" (DWM 383).

30 Sat   Holy Saturday   Violet / White
DWM Liturgy of the Word 384 (optional)

Easter Vigil

DWM 391 Gloria, Creed

Lec 41: Use at least three, or up to seven readings from the OT, but always include #3: 1) Gn 1:1-2:2 or 1, 26-31a; 2) Gn 22:1-18 or 1-2, 9a, 10-13, 15-18; 3) Ex 14:15-15:1; 4) Is 54:5-14; 5) Is 55:1-11; 6) Bar 3:9-15, 32-4:4; 7) Ez 36:16-17a, 18-28 ♦ RSV2CE Psalms are given in DWM. Coverdale Psalms after each OT Reading follow: 1) Ps 104:1-2, 5-6, 10-14, 24, 30, 36 or Ps 33:3-7, 12-13, 19, 21; 2) Ps 16:1, 6, 9-12; 3) Cantemus Domino (DWDO 77); 4) Ps 30:1, 3-5, 11-13; 5) Ecce Deus

(DWDO 74); 6) Ps 19:7-10; 7) Ps 42:1-2, 4-5, 43:3-4 or Ps 51:10-13, 16-17 ♦ NT
Reading: Rom 6:3-11 Psalm after the Epistle: Responsorial RSV2CE: Ps 118:1-2,
15c-17, 22-23 [refrain: triple "Alleluia"]; or Coverdale Psalm: Ps 118:1-2, 16-17,
22-23 [triple "Alleluia" before and after] ♦ Mk 16:1-7

> ¶ "Of this night's Vigil, which is the greatest and most noble of all solemnities, there is to be only one celebration in each church. The Easter Vigil consists of four parts. It is arranged in such a way that after the Lucernarium and Easter Proclamation (first part), Holy Church meditates on the wonders the Lord God has done for his people from the beginning (second part), until, as day approaches, with new members reborn in Baptism (third part), the Church is called to the table the Lord has prepared for his people, the memorial of his Death and Resurrection until he comes again (fourth part). The entire celebration must take place at night, beginning after nightfall and ending before daybreak" (DWM 391).
>
> ¶ "In this Vigil, nine lessons are provided, seven from the Old Testament and two from the New Testament (the Epistle and the Gospel), all of which should be read whenever this can be done so that the character of the Vigil, which demands an extended period of time, may be preserved. Where pastoral reasons suggest it, the number of lessons from the Old Testament may be reduced, always bearing in mind that the reading of the Word of God is a fundamental aspect of the Easter Vigil. At least three lessons should be read from the Old Testament, both from the Law and the Prophets; and their respective Psalms, or the equivalent texts from the Coverdale Psalter, should be sung. An appropriate hymn may replace one of the Psalms. Never should the reading of chapter 14 of Exodus with its canticle be omitted" (DWM 406).

MP Pss: 88   Lessons: Zec 9:9-12 ♦ 1 Pt 2:21-end
EP 1 of EASTER
    Pss: 27   Lessons: Jb 19:21-27 ♦ Jn 2:13-22

31 SUN   EASTER DAY *Solemnity*   White
DWM 430 Gloria, Creed
Lec 42, 41: Acts 10:34a, 37-43 ♦ Col 3:1-4 or 1 Cor 5:6b-8 ♦ Jn 20:1-9 (no. 42) or
Mt 28:1-10 (no. 41); or, at an afternoon or evening Mass, Lk 24:13-35 (no. 46)

> ¶ "The Sequence *Victimae paschali laudes* may be sung or said" after the Alleluia verse (DWM 430).
>
> ¶ "In Easter Sunday Masses which are celebrated with a congregation, the rite of renewal of baptismal promises may take place after the homily, according to the text used at the Easter Vigil (p. 425). In this case, the [Nicene] Creed is omitted" (DWM 431).

MP Pss: 148-150   Lessons: Ex 12:1-14 ♦ Rv 1:4-18   Te Deum
EP 2   113-114 or 118   Ex 14:5-end ♦ Jn 20:11-23

> ¶ *Regina Caeli* may be said after EP or Compline during Eastertide until First Evensong of Trinity Sunday.

April 2024

1 Mon   MONDAY IN THE OCTAVE OF EASTER *Solemnity*   White
DWM 432 Gloria, Creed
Lec 261: Acts 2:14, 22-33 ♦ Mt 28:8-15

> ¶ "The first eight days of Easter Time constitute the Octave of Easter and are celebrated as Solemnities of the Lord" (*Universal Norms on the Liturgical Year and the Calendar*, § 24).
> ¶ "The Sequence *Victimae paschali laudes*, pp. 430-431, may be said throughout the Octave" after the Alleluia verse (DWM 432).

	MP Pss:	Lessons:		
MP	93, 98	Ex 15:1-18 ♦ Lk 24:1-12	Te Deum
EP	66	Is 12 ♦ Rv 7:9-end	

2 Tue   TUESDAY IN THE OCTAVE OF EASTER *Solemnity*   White
DWM 434 Gloria, Creed
Lec 262: Acts 2:36-41 ♦ Jn 20:11-18

		Lessons:	
MP	Pss: 103	Is 25:1-9 ♦ 1 Pt 1:1-12	Te Deum
EP	111, 114	Is 26:1-19 ♦ Mt 28:1-15	

3 Wed   WEDNESDAY IN THE OCTAVE OF EASTER *Solemnity*   White
DWM 436 Gloria, Creed
Lec 263: Acts 3:1-10 ♦ Lk 24:13-35

		Lessons:	
MP	Pss: 97, 99	Is 61 ♦ 1 Pt 1:13-end	Te Deum
EP	115	Sg 2:8-end ♦ Mt 28:16-end	

4 Thu   THURSDAY IN THE OCTAVE OF EASTER *Solemnity*   White
DWM 438 Gloria, Creed
Lec 264: Acts 3:11-26 ♦ Lk 24:35-48

		Lessons:	
MP	Pss: 146-147	Jb 14:1-15 ♦ 1 Thes 4:13-end	Te Deum
EP	148-149	Dn 12 ♦ Mk 16	

5 Fri   FRIDAY IN THE OCTAVE OF EASTER *Solemnity*   White
DWM 440 Gloria, Creed
Lec 265: Acts 4:1-12 ♦ Jn 21:1-14

		Lessons:	
MP	Pss: 136	Zep 3:14-end ♦ Acts 17:16-31	Te Deum
EP	118	2 Kgs 4:8-37 ♦ Lk 7:11-17	

April 2024

> ¶ Today being a *Solemnity*, the obligation to abstain from meat or to perform some other penitential act is dispensed (CIC 1251).

6 Sat SATURDAY IN THE OCTAVE OF EASTER *Solemnity* White
DWM 442 Gloria, Creed
Lec 266: Acts 4:13-21 ♦ Mk 16:9-15

MP Pss: 145 Lessons: Jer 31:1-14 ♦ Acts 26:1-23 Te Deum
EP 1 of The Second Sunday of Easter
Pss: 104 Lessons: Mi 7:7-end ♦ Jn 21:15-end

7 SUN SECOND SUNDAY OF EASTER *Solemnity*
Octave Day of Easter (Divine Mercy Sunday) White
DWM 444 Gloria, Creed
Lec 44: Acts 4:32-35 ♦ Ps 118:1-4, 13-15, 22-24 ♦ 1 Jn 5:1-7 ♦ Jn 20:19-31

> ¶ "The Rite of Sprinkling Holy Water (Appendix 2) as a memorial of Baptism may precede the principal Sunday Mass and is especially fitting on the Sundays in Eastertide. When the Rite of Sprinkling Holy Water takes place, the Priest may wear a cope in the colour of the day before changing into the vestments for Mass. The Introit may follow directly and Mass continues with the *Kyrie*" (DWM 124, 1044). Cf. the rubric at DWM 1045 which says that, after the Rite of Sprinkling, "Mass continues with the Collect for Purity."

MP Pss: 146-147 Lessons: Ez 37:1-14 ♦ Lk 24:13-35 Te Deum
EP 2 111-113 1 Kgs 17:8-end ♦ Lk 24:36-49

8 Mon ANNUNCIATION OF THE LORD *Solemnity* White
DWM 707 Gloria, Creed
Lec 545: Is 7:10-14; 8:10 ♦ Ps 40:8-13 ♦ Heb 10:4-10 ♦ Lk 1:26-38

MP Pss: 85, 87 Lessons: Is 52:7-12 ♦ Heb 2:5-end Te Deum
EP 110, 132 1 Sm 2:1-10 ♦ Mt 1:18-23

9 Tue Eastertide Feria White
DWM 444
Lec 268: Acts 4:32-37 ♦ Jn 3:7b-15

MP Pss: 5-6 Lessons: Dt 2:1-25 ♦ Acts 2:1-21
EP 10-11 Dt 2:26-3:5 ♦ Acts 2:22-end

10 Wed   Eastertide Feria   White
DWM 444
Lec 269: Acts 5:17-26 ♦ Jn 3:16-21

MP Pss: 119:I-III   Lessons: Dt 3:18-end ♦ Acts 3:1-4:4
EP   12-14   Dt 4:1-24 ♦ Acts 4:5-31

11 Thu   Saint Stanislaus, Bishop and Martyr *Memorial*   Red
DWM 712
Lec 270: Acts 5:27-33 ♦ Jn 3:31-36
    Or:
Lec 550: Rv 12:10-12a (#714.3) ♦ Jn 17:11b-19 (#718.7)

MP Pss: 18:I   Lessons: Dt 4:25-40 ♦ Acts 4:32-5:11
EP   18:II   Dt 5:1-21 ♦ Acts 5:12-end

12 Fri   Eastertide Feria   White
DWM 444
Lec 271: Acts 5:34-42 ♦ Jn 6:1-15

MP Pss: 16-17   Lessons: Dt 5:22-end ♦ Acts 6:1-7:16
EP   134-135   Dt 6 ♦ Acts 7:17-34

13 Sat   Eastertide Feria   White
    Or:
    St Martin I, Pope and Martyr   *Red*
    BVM: Mass of Saint Mary 4   *White*
DWM 444
Lec 272: Acts 6:1-7 ♦ Jn 6:16-21
    Or, for St Martin I, Pope and Martyr: DWM 712
Lec 551: 2 Tm 2:8-13; 3:10-12 (#716.5) ♦ Jn 15:18-21 (#718.6)
    Or, for Saint Mary: DWM 994
Lec 707-712 any readings from the Common of the BVM

MP Pss: 20-21   Lessons: Dt 7:1-11 ♦ Acts 7:35-8:4
EP 1 of The Third Sunday of Easter
    Pss: 110, 116-117   Lessons: Dt 7:12-end ♦ Acts 8:4-25

14 SUN   THIRD SUNDAY OF EASTER   White
DWM 446 Gloria, Creed
Lec 47: Acts 3:13-15, 17-19ab ♦ Ps 4:1, 3, 6-7 ♦ 1 Jn 2:1-5a ♦ Lk 24:35-48

MP	Pss: 148-150	Lessons: Is 55 ♦ Mk 5:21-end Te Deum
EP 2	114-115	Dt 4:25-40 ♦ Rv 2:1-17

15 Mon   Eastertide Feria   White

DWM 446

Lec 273: Acts 6:8-15 ♦ Jn 6:22-29

MP	Pss: 25	Lessons: Dt 8 ♦ Acts 8:26-end
EP	9, 15	Dt 9:1-10 ♦ Acts 9:1-31

16 Tue   Eastertide Feria   White

DWM 446

Lec 274: Acts 7:51-8:1a ♦ Jn 6:30-35

MP	Pss: 26, 28	Lessons: Dt 9:11-end ♦ Acts 9:32-end
EP	36, 39	Dt 10 ♦ Acts 10:1-23

17 Wed   Eastertide Feria   White

Or:

Can: *St Kateri Tekakwitha, Virgin*   *White*

DWM 446

Lec 275: Acts 8:1b-8 ♦ Jn 6:35-40

Or, for St Kateri Tekakwitha, Virgin: DWM 779

MP	Pss: 38	Lessons: Dt 11:1-12 ♦ Acts 10:24-end
EP	119:IV-VI	Dt 11:13-end ♦ Acts 11:1-18

18 Thu   Eastertide Feria   White

Or:

Can: *Bl Marie-Anne Blondin, Virgin*   *White*

DWM 446

Lec 276: Acts 8:26-40 ♦ Jn 6:44-51

Or, for Bl Marie-Anne Blondin, Virgin: DWM 938

MP	Pss: 37:I	Lessons: Dt 12:1-14 ♦ Acts 11:19-end
EP	37:II	Dt 15:1-18 ♦ Acts 12:1-24

19 Fri   Eastertide Feria   White

DWM 446

Lec 277: Acts 9:1-20 ♦ Jn 6:52-59

MP	Pss: 105:I	Lessons: Dt 16:1-20 ♦ Acts 12:25-13:12
EP	105:II	Dt 17:8-end ♦ Acts 13:13-43

20 Sat	Eastertide Feria	White
	Or:	
	BVM: Mass of Saint Mary 4	*White*
	DWM 446	
	Lec 278: Acts 9:31-42 ♦ Jn 6:60-69	
	Or, for Saint Mary: DWM 994	
	Lec 707-712 any readings from the Common of the BVM	

MP Pss: 30, 32   Lessons: Dt 18:9-end ♦ Acts 13:44-14:7
EP 1 of The Fourth Sunday of Easter
      Pss: 42-43   Lessons: Dt 19 ♦ Acts 14:8-end

21 SUN	FOURTH SUNDAY OF EASTER COMMONLY CALLED GOOD SHEPHERD SUNDAY	White
	DWM 448 Gloria, Creed	
	Lec 50: Acts 4:8-12 ♦ Ps 118:1, 8-9, 21-23, 26, 28-29 ♦ 1 Jn 3:1-2 ♦ Jn 10:11-18	

MP Pss: 63, 98   Lessons: Nm 13:1-2,17-end ♦ Lk   Te Deum
                                            7:11-17
EP 2   103   Dt 5:1-21 ♦ Rv 2:18-3:6

22 Mon	Eastertide Feria	White
	DWM 448	
	Lec 279: Acts 11:1-18 ♦ Jn 10:1-10	

MP Pss: 41, 52   Lessons: Dt 21:22-22:8 ♦ Acts 15:1-21
EP   44   Dt 24:5-end ♦ Acts 15:22-35

23 Tue	Saint George, Martyr *Memorial*	Red
	DWM 715	
	Lec 280: Acts 11:19-26 ♦ Jn 10:22-30	
	Or:	
	Lec 553: Rv 21:5-7 (#714.4) ♦ Lk 9:23-26 (#718.4)	

MP Pss: 45   Lessons: Dt 26 ♦ Acts 15:36-16:5
EP   47-48   Dt 28:58-end ♦ Acts 16:6-end

24 Wed	Eastertide Feria	White
	Or:	
	St Adalbert, Bishop and Martyr	*Red*
	St Fidelis of Sigmaringen, Priest and Martyr	*Red*
	DWM 448	

Lec 281: Acts 12:24-13:5a ♦ Jn 12:44-50
> *Or, for St Adalbert, Bishop and Martyr:* DWM 717

Lec 553A: 2 Cor 6:4-10 (#716.4) ♦ Jn 10:11-16 (#724.10)
> *Or, for St Fidelis of Sigmaringen, Priest and Martyr:* DWM 716

Lec 554: Col 1:24-29 (#722.9) ♦ Jn 17:20-26 (#742.26)

MP	Pss: 119:VII-IX	Lessons: Dt 29:10-end ♦ Acts 17:1-15	
EP	49, 53	Dt 30 ♦ Acts 17:16-end	

25 Thu Saint Mark, Evangelist *Feast* — Red

DWM 718 Gloria

Lec 555: 1 Pt 5:5b-14 ♦ Ps 89:1-2, 5-6, 16-17 ♦ Mk 16:15-20

MP	Pss: 145	Lessons: Sir 51:13-end ♦ Acts 15:35-end	Te Deum
EP	67, 96	Is 62:6-10 ♦ 2 Tm 4:1-11	

26 Fri Eastertide Feria — White
Or:
Can: *Our Lady of Good Counsel* — *White*

DWM 448

Lec 283: Acts 13:26-33 ♦ Jn 14:1-6
> *Or, for Our Lady of Good Counsel:* DWM 913

Lec 707-712 any reading from the Common of the Blessed Virgin Mary

MP	Pss: 40, 54	Lessons: Dt 31:30-32:14 ♦ Acts 19:8-20
EP	51	Dt 32:15-47 ♦ Acts 19:21-end

27 Sat Eastertide Feria — White
Or:
BVM: Mass of Saint Mary 4 — *White*

DWM 448

Lec 284: Acts 13:44-52 ♦ Jn 14:7-14
> *Or, for Saint Mary:* DWM 994

Lec 707-712 any readings from the Common of the BVM

MP	Pss: 55	Lessons: Dt 33 ♦ Acts 20:1-16

EP 1 of The Fifth Sunday of Easter

	Pss: 138-139	Lessons: Dt 32:48-end, 34:1-end ♦ Acts 20:17-end

28 SUN   FIFTH SUNDAY OF EASTER   White
DWM 450 Gloria, Creed
Lec 53: Acts 9:26-31 ♦ Ps 22:25-27, 30-32 ♦ 1 Jn 3:18-24 ♦ Jn 15:1-8

MP Pss: 24, 29   Lessons: Nm 22:1-35 ♦ Jn 11:1-44   Te Deum
EP 2   8, 84   Dt 10:12-11:1 ♦ Rv 3:7-end

29 Mon   Saint Catherine of Siena, Virgin and Doctor of the Church *Memorial*   White
DWM 721
Lec 285: Acts 14:5-18 ♦ Jn 14:21-26
    Or:
Lec 557: 1 Jn 1:5-2:2 ♦ Mt 11:25-30 (#742.4)

MP Pss: 56-58   Lessons: Jos 1 ♦ Acts 21:1-16
EP   64-65   Jos 2 ♦ Acts 21:17-36

30 Tue   Eastertide Feria   White
          Or:
          USA: *St Pius V, Pope*   *White*
          Can: *St Marie of the Incarnation, Religious*   *White*
DWM 450
Lec 286: Acts 14:19-28 ♦ Jn 14:27-31a
    Or, for St Pius V, Pope: DWM 722
Lec 558: 1 Cor 4:1-5 (#722.3) ♦ Jn 21:15-17 (#724.12)
    Or, for St Marie of the Incarnation, Religious: DWM 944

MP Pss: 61-62   Lessons: Jos 3 ♦ Acts 21:37-22:22
EP   68   Jos 4:1-5:1 ♦ Acts 22:23-23:11

May 2024

1 Wed   Eastertide Feria   White
           Or:
           St Joseph the Worker   *White*
           Can: *St Pius V, Pope*   *White*
DWM 450
Lec 287: Acts 15:1-6 ♦ Jn 15:1-8
    Or, for St Joseph the Worker: DWM 723
Lec 559: Gn 1:26-2:3 or Col 3:14-15, 17, 23-24 ♦ **Mt 13:54-58**
    Or, for St Pius V, Pope: DWM 722
Lec 558: 1 Cor 4:1-5 (#722.3) ♦ Jn 21:15-17 (#724.12)

MP   Pss: 72   Lessons: Jos 5:13-6:20 ♦ Acts 23:12-end
EP   119:X-XII   Jos 7 ♦ Acts 24:1-23

2 Thu   Saint Athanasius, Bishop and Doctor of the Church *Memorial*   White
DWM 724
Lec 288: Acts 15:7-21 ♦ Jn 15:9-11
    Or:
Lec 560: 1 Jn 5:1-5 (#716.10) ♦ Mt 10:22-25a

MP   Pss: 70-71   Lessons: Jos 9:3-end ♦ Acts 24:24-25:12
EP   74   Jos 10:1-15 ♦ Acts 25:13-end

3 Fri   Saints Philip and James, Apostles *Feast*   Red
DWM 725 Gloria
Lec 561: 1 Cor 15:1-8 ♦ Ps 19:1-4 ♦ Jn 14:6-14

MP   Pss: 119:XVIII-XX   Lessons: Prv 4:10-18 ♦ Jn 6:1-14   Te Deum
EP   139 or 119:IV-V   Jb 23:1-12 or Is 30:15-21 ♦ Jn 1:43-end or Jn 17:1-8

4 Sat   The English Martyrs *Memorial*   Red
DWM 726
Lec 290: Acts 16:1-10 ♦ Jn 15:18-21

MP   Pss: 75-76   Lessons: Jos 23 ♦ Acts 28:1-15
EP 1 of The Sixth Sunday of Easter
       Pss: 23, 27   Lessons: Jos 24:1-28 ♦ Acts 28:16-end

5 SUN   SIXTH SUNDAY OF EASTER COMMONLY CALLED ROGATION   White
SUNDAY

DWM 452 Gloria, Creed

Lec 56: Acts 10:25-26, 34-35, 44-48 ♦ Ps 98:1-5 ♦ 1 Jn 4:7-10 ♦ Jn 15:9-17

> ¶ Where it is the custom, joyful Rogation Sunday processions may take place before or after the principal Sunday Mass. They may be accompanied by hymns praising the beauty of creation and other hymns appropriate to a Sunday in Eastertide. The Litany of the Saints (DWM 411) may be used in procession.
>
> ¶ On the Rogation Days (which are the three weekdays before the celebration of Ascension Day), The Litany may be sung or said in procession. (DWM 1061).

MP	Pss: 93, 96	Lessons:	Nm 22:36-23:12 ♦ Rom 6:1-14	Te Deum
EP 2	34		Dt 28:1-14 ♦ Mk 4:1-20	

6 Mon   Rogation Day   White

[Can: *St John the Apostle in Eastertide*]

[Can: *St François de Laval, Bishop*]

DWM 454

Lec 291: Acts 16:11-15 ♦ Jn 15:26-16:4a

St John the Apostle in Eastertide may optionally be commemorated only in the Daily Office by adding the DWM 728 Collect after the Collect of the Day.

St François de Laval, Bishop may optionally be commemorated only in the Daily Office by adding the DWM 928 Collect after the Collect of the Day.

> ¶ Though inscribed in the Canadian National Calendar as an *Obligatory Memorial*, the liturgical observance of St François de Laval is here listed as an *Optional Memorial*, in deference to the Ordinariate's Particular Calendar and to permit the celebration of St John the Apostle in Eastertide.

MP	Pss: 80	Lessons:	Dt 7:6-13 ♦ Mt 6:5-18
EP	77, 79		Dt 8 ♦ Mt 6:19-end

7 Tue   Rogation Day   White

DWM 454

Lec 292: Acts 16:22-34 ♦ Jn 16:5-11

MP	Pss: 78:I	Lessons:	Dt 11:8-21 ♦ Lk 5:1-11
EP	78:II		1 Kgs 8:22-43 ♦ Jas 5:1-18

8 Wed   Rogation Day   White

[Can: *Bl Catherine of Saint Augustine, Virgin*]

DWM 454

Lec 293: Acts 17:15, 22-18:1 ♦ Jn 16:12-15

Bl Catherine of Saint Augustine, Virgin may optionally be commemorated only in the Daily Office by adding the DWM 938 Collect after the Collect of the Day.

MP Pss: 119:XIII-XV   Lessons: Jl 2:21-27 ♦ Jn 6:22-40
EP 1 of the Ascension
    Pss: 68:1-20   Lessons: Dn 3:29-37 (Song of the Three Children
                                        29-37) or Ez 1:4-5,26-end ♦ Mt 28:16-end
                                        or Mk 16:14-19

> ¶ The Song of the Three Children appears in the third Chapter of Daniel. The verse numbering differs in various editions of the Bible because of the Song being one of the deuterocanonical portions of Daniel. In the RSV-CE and RSV-2CE, the Song appears italicized between Daniel 3:23 and Daniel 3:24. It is numbered as verses 1-68 and is followed by verses 24-30. The appointed verses are numbered *29-37* within the italicized section, and correspond to the Canticle *Benedictus es, Domine* ("Blessed art thou, O Lord, God of our fathers...") plus the first three verses of the Canticle *Benedicite, Omnia Opera Domine*. In the *Nova Vulgata*, NRSV-CE, and some other bibles the appointed verses are Dn 3:52-59.

9 Thu   ASCENSION OF THE LORD *Solemnity* HDO   White
        Vigil (Ascension Eve):
DWM 456 Gloria, Creed
        On the Day:
DWM 458 Gloria, Creed
Lec 58: Acts 1:1-11 ♦ Ps 47:1-2, 5-8 ♦ Eph 4:1-13 or 4:1-7, 11-13 or Eph 1:17-23 ♦
Mk 16:15-20

> ¶ The Paschal Candle remains illuminated until the conclusion of Eastertide after the dismissal of the last Mass of Pentecost Day (DWM 473).
>
> ¶ On the Solemnity of the Ascension, the first reading is the same in all years of the three year cycle. Options are provided for the second reading, which may be either the reading proper to Year B or the reading proper to Year A. The Gospel is always proper to the specific year. The second reading for Year B is cited first above in both a long and short form. It may be replaced with the reading for Year A, cited last. Sacristans and Readers should consult with the Celebrant or Homilist to ascertain the desired reading before setting the book and before reading.

MP Pss: 8, 47   Lessons: 2 Kgs 2:1-15 ♦ Jn 17   Te Deum
EP 2   24, 96   2 Sm 23:1-5 ♦ Heb 1

10 Fri   Ascensiontide Feria   White
        Or:
        St Damien de Veuster, Priest   *White*
        St John De Avila, Priest and Doctor of the Church   *White*
DWM 452
Lec 295: Acts 18:9-18 ♦ Jn 16:20-23a
        Or, for St Damien de Veuster, Priest: DWM 729

Or, for St John De Avila, Priest and Doctor of the Church: DWM 936

MP Pss: 85-86   Lessons: Jgs 2:6-end ♦ Heb 2
EP   91-92   Jgs 4 ♦ Heb 3

11 Sat   The Blessed Virgin Mary, Mother of the Church *Memorial*   White
DWM 913
Lec 296: Acts 18:23-28 ♦ Jn 16:23b-28
        Or:
Lec 689: Gen 3:9-15, 20 or Lec 708.1: Acts 1:12-14 ♦ Lec 712.12: Jn 19:25-27 but
add vv 28-34

❖ The Ordinariate will observe the Memorial of The Blessed Virgin Mary, Mother of the Church, on the Saturday after Ascension Day. This Memorial has a precedence higher than any other Memorial, but lower than all Feasts, Solemnities, and privileged Octaves. The General Roman Calendar observes the Memorial on Whitmonday. The move within the Ordinariate to the Saturday after Ascension Day prevents the Memorial from being permanently occluded by the higher ranking day within the Octave of Pentecost.

¶ The proper readings are taken from the Lectionary as indicated above. For the Gospel reading, vv 25-28 are to be taken from the Lectionary, with vv 29-34 added from the RSV-2CE translation of the bible. The minor propers are taken from the Common of the Blessed Virgin Mary (DWM 913). The Divine Worship form of the Collect of the Day follows:

O God, Father of mercies,
whose Only Begotten Son, whilst nailed upon the Cross,
did choose the Blessed Virgin Mary, his own Mother,
to be our Mother also:
grant, we beseech thee, that, with the assistance of her charity,
thy Church, made more fruitful day by day
may exult in the holiness of her offspring,
may draw to her embrace all the families of the peoples;
through the same Jesus Christ thy Son our Lord,
who liveth and reigneth with thee, in the unity of the Holy Spirit,
ever one God, world without end. Amen.

¶ At Morning Prayer, the Antiphon for the Benedictus is "The disciples devoted themselves with one accord * to prayer with Mary, the Mother of Jesus." At Mattins the Office hymn is "Quae caritatis fulgidum" or "O virgo mater, filia" taken from the Office of Readings.

¶ Because this Memorial is observed on Saturday in the Ordinariate, Evening Prayer is always EP1 of the Sunday following. The Antiphon for the Magnificat proper to this memorial will not normally be used, but is provided here for informational purposes: "The Lord said to his mother: * Woman, behold thy son. And to the disciple: * Behold thy mother." Likewise, the evening office hymns, "Virgo, mater Ecclesiae" or "Ave, Maris Stella" will also not normally be used.

MP Pss: 87, 90   Lessons: Jgs 5 ♦ Heb 4:1-13
EP 1 of The Seventh Sunday of Easter
        Pss: 136   Lessons: Jgs 6:1-24 ♦ Heb 4:15-5:10

| 12 SUN | SEVENTH SUNDAY OF EASTER | | White |

DWM 460 Gloria, Creed

Lec 60: Acts 1:15-17, 20a, 20c-26 ♦ Ps 103:1-2, 11-12, 19-20 ♦ 1 Jn 4:11-16 ♦ Jn 17:11b-19

| MP | Pss: 66-67 | Lessons: | Is 52:1-12 ♦ Eph 4:1-16 | Te Deum |
| EP 2 | 19, 46 | | Is 62 ♦ Rv 5 | |

| 13 Mon | Eastertide Feria | | White |

Or:

Our Lady of Fatima — *White*

DWM 460

Lec 297: Acts 19:1-8 ♦ Jn 16:29-33

    Or, for Our Lady of Fatima: DWM 730

Lec 707-712 any reading from the Common of the Blessed Virgin Mary

| MP | Pss: 89:I | Lessons: | Jgs 6:25-end ♦ Heb 5:11-6:end |
| EP | 89:II | | Jgs 7 ♦ Heb 7 |

| 14 Tue | Saint Matthias, Apostle *Feast* | | Red |

DWM 731 Gloria

Lec 564: Acts 1:15-17, 20-26 ♦ Ps 113:1-7 ♦ Jn 15:9-17

| MP | Pss: 80 | Lessons: | Is 22:15-22 ♦ Mt 7:15-27 | Te Deum |
| EP | 33 or 48, 122 | | 1 Sm 16:1-13 or 1 Sm 2:27-35 ♦ 1 Cor 4:1-8 or Mt 11:25-end | |

| 15 Wed | Eastertide Feria | | White |

Or:

St Isidore — *White*

DWM 460

Lec 299: Acts 20:28-38 ♦ Jn 17:11b-19

    Or, for St Isidore: DWM 733

| MP | Pss: 101, 109 | Lessons: | Jgs 13 ♦ Heb 9:15-end |
| EP | 119:XVI-XVIII | | Jgs 14 ♦ Heb 10:1-18 |

| 16 Thu | Eastertide Feria | | White |

DWM 460

Lec 300: Acts 22:30; 23:6-11 ♦ Jn 17:20-26

MP Pss: 105:I   Lessons: Jgs 16:4-end ♦ Heb 10:19-end
EP   105:II   Ru 1 ♦ Heb 11

17 Fri   Eastertide Feria   White
DWM 460
Lec 301: Acts 25:13b-21 ♦ Jn 21:15-19

MP Pss: 102   Lessons: Ru 2 ♦ Heb 12:1-13
EP   107:I   Ru 3 ♦ Heb 12:14-end

18 Sat   Eastertide Feria   White
Or:
St John I, Pope and Martyr   *Red*
BVM: Mass of Saint Mary 4   *White*
DWM 460
Lec 302: Acts 28:16-20, 30-31 ♦ Jn 21:20-25
     Or, for St John I, Pope and Martyr: DWM 733
Lec 565: Rv 3:14b, 20-22 (#738.2) ♦ Lk 22:24-30 (#724.9)
     Or, for Saint Mary: DWM 994
Lec 707-712 any readings from the Common of the BVM

MP Pss: 107:II, 108   Lessons: Ru 4:1-17 ♦ Heb 13
EP 1 of PENTECOST
     Pss: 33   Lessons: Gn 11:1-9 ♦ Acts 18:24-19:7

19 SUN   THE DAY OF PENTECOST COMMONLY CALLED WHITSUNDAY   Red
     Solemnity
     <u>Vigil (Whitsun Eve):</u>
DWM 462 Extended Vigil: Gloria, Renewal of Baptismal Promises
DWM 468 Vigil Mass: Gloria, Creed
OT Readings: Lec 62: Gn 11:1-9 ♦ Ex 19:3-8a, 16-20b ♦ Ez 37:1-14 ♦ Jl 2:28-32.
In the extended form of the Vigil, all four OT readings are read, each followed by the Tracts listed in DWM 462.
Vigil Mass alone: Use one OT Reading followed by Ps 104:1-2, 24, 27-30.
Epistle and Gospel: Lec 62: Rom 8:22-27 ♦ Jn 7:37-39

¶ Fifty Days after the Easter Vigil, the Extended Vigil of Pentecost may afford a suitable occasion for administering the Sacraments of Initiation: "After the homily, if there is anyone to be baptised, received into full communion with the Catholic Church, or confirmed, the sacramental rites are administered as set out in *Divine Worship: Occasional Services* and as directed at the Easter Vigil" (DWM 465).

¶ "The extended form of the Vigil of Pentecost may be celebrated on the Saturday evening, either before or after first Evening Prayer of Pentecost Sunday. Red vestments are worn for the Masses of Pentecost, though the Priest may wear a white cope for the extended Vigil up to and including the sprinkling with holy water. The Paschal Candle and the candles of the altar remain lighted throughout the Vigil" (DWM 462).

On the Day:

DWM 471 Gloria, Creed

Lec 63: Acts 2:1-11 ♦ Ps 104:1, 24, 29, 30, 31, 34 ♦ Gal 5:16-25 or 1 Cor 12:3b-7, 12-13 ♦ Jn 15:26-27; 16:12-15 or Jn 20:19-23

¶ Note that DWM prescribes a genuflection at the Alleluia *Emitte Spiritum*: "Come, Holy Ghost, *[Here genuflect]* and fill the hearts of thy faithful people ..." (DWM 471), as also at the Alleluia through Whitsun Week.

¶ "The Sequence *Veni, Sancte Spiritus* may be sung or said" after the Alleluia verse (DWM 471).

¶ At the end of the last Mass of Pentecost Day: "With Eastertide now concluded, the Paschal Candle is extinguished. It is desirable to keep the Paschal Candle in the baptistery with due honour so that it is lit at the celebration of Baptism and the candles of those baptised are lit from it" (DWM 473).

¶ On Whitsunday, the first reading is the same in all years of the three year cycle. Options are provided for the second reading and the Gospel, which may be either the readings proper to Year B or the readings proper to Year A. The readings for Year B are cited first above. They may be replaced with the readings for Year A, which are cited last. Sacristans and Readers should consult with the Celebrant or Homilist to ascertain the desired reading before setting the book and before reading.

MP	Pss: 118	Lessons: Jl 2:28-end ♦ Rom 8:1-17	Te Deum
EP 2	145	Is 11:1-9 ♦ Rom 8:18-end	

20 Mon	Monday in Whitsun Week	Red

[*St Bernardine of Siena, Priest*]

DWM 474 Gloria

Lec 341: Jas 3:13-18 ♦ Mk 9:14-29 (Ordinary Time Week 7 readings)

Or Lec 63 or Lec 1001: readings from the Mass of Pentecost may be repeated, or readings may be taken from those for Confirmation, nos. 764-768, as used for Votive Masses of the Holy Spirit

Or, for St Bernardine of Siena, Priest: DWM 735 – if commemorated, Collect only

May 2024

> ¶ "The Sequence *Veni, Sancte Spiritus,* pp. 471-472, may be said" after the Alleluia verse on each day of Whitsun Week (DWM 474).
>
> ❖ Because Pentecost has a privileged Octave in the calendar of the Ordinariate, the Memorial of The Blessed Virgin Mary, Mother of the Church, is observed on the Saturday after Ascension Day. Other memorials and optional memorials falling during the Octave of Pentecost, if observed at all, are commemorated with a collect only, in the manner described in GIRM 355 (DWM 133, 104).

MP	Pss: 106:I	Lessons:	Ez 11:14-20 ♦ Acts 2:12-36	Te Deum
EP	106:II		Wis 1:1-7 ♦ Acts 2:37-end	

21 Tue — Tuesday in Whitsun Week — Red
[*St Christopher Magallanes, Priest, and Companions, Martyrs*]
[Can: *St Eugène de Mazenod, Bishop*]
DWM 476 Gloria
Lec 342: Jas 4:1-10 ♦ Mk 9:30-37 (Ordinary Time Week 7 readings)
> Or Lec 63 or Lec 1001: readings from the Mass of Pentecost may be repeated, or readings may be taken from those for Confirmation, nos. 764-768, as used for Votive Masses of the Holy Spirit
> *Or, for St Christopher Magallanes, Priest, and Companions, Martyrs:* DWM 735 – if commemorated, Collect only
> *Or, for St Eugène de Mazenod, Bishop:* DWM 940 – if commemorated, Collect only

MP	Pss: 120-123	Lessons:	Ez 37:1-14 ♦ 1 Cor 12:1-13	Te Deum
EP	124-127		Wis 7:15-8:1 ♦ 1 Cor 12:27-13:end	

22 Wed — Ember Wednesday in Whitsun Week — Red
[*St Rita of Cascia, Religious*]
DWM 478 Gloria
Lec 343: Jas 4:13-17 ♦ Mk 9:38-40 (Ordinary Time Week 7 readings)
> Or Lec 63 or Lec 1001: readings from the Mass of Pentecost may be repeated, or readings may be taken from those for Confirmation, nos. 764-768, as used for Votive Masses of the Holy Spirit
St Rita of Cascia, Religious may optionally be commemorated only in the Daily Office by adding the DWM 736 Collect after the Collect of the Day.

MP	Pss: 119:XIX-XXII	Lessons:	1 Kgs 19:1-18 ♦ 1 Cor 2	Te Deum
EP	128-130		Wis 9 ♦ 1 Cor 3	

23 Thu — Thursday in Whitsun Week — Red
DWM 480 Gloria
Lec 344: Jas 5:1-6 ♦ Mk 9:41-50 (Ordinary Time Week 7 readings)

May 2024

Or Lec 63 or Lec 1001: readings from the Mass of Pentecost may be repeated, or readings may be taken from those for Confirmation, nos. 764-768, as used for Votive Masses of the Holy Spirit

MP	Pss: 131-133	Lessons: 2 Sm 23:1-5 ♦ Eph 6:10-20	Te Deum
EP	134-135	Ex 35:30-36:1 ♦ Gal 5:13-end	

24 Fri Ember Friday in Whitsun Week Red
[Can: *Bl Louis-Zéphirin Moreau, Bishop*]

DWM 482 Gloria

Lec 345: Jas 5:9-12 ♦ Mk 10:1-12 (Ordinary Time Week 7 readings)

Or Lec 63 or Lec 1001: readings from the Mass of Pentecost may be repeated, or readings may be taken from those for Confirmation, nos. 764-768, as used for Votive Masses of the Holy Spirit

Bl Louis-Zéphirin Moreau, Bishop may optionally be commemorated only in the Daily Office by adding the DWM 940 Collect after the Collect of the Day.

MP	Pss: 140, 142	Lessons: Nm 11:16-17,24-29 ♦ 2 Cor 5:14-6:10	Te Deum
EP	141, 143	Jer 31:31-34 ♦ 2 Cor 3	

25 Sat Ember Saturday in Whitsun Week Red
[*St Bede the Venerable, Priest and Doctor of the Church*]
[*St Gregory VII, Pope*]
[*St Mary Magdalene de' Pazzi, Virgin*]

DWM 484 Gloria

Lec 346: Jas 5:13-20 ♦ Mk 10:13-16 (Ordinary Time Week 7 readings)

Or Lec 63, Lec 827-831, or Lec 857-861: readings from the Mass of Pentecost may be repeated or readings may be taken from For Holy Church, nos. 827-832, or from those For Vocations to Holy Orders or Religious Life, nos. 857-861

St Bede the Venerable, Priest and Doctor of the Church may optionally be commemorated only in the Daily Office by adding the DWM 739 Collect after the Collect of the Day.

St Gregory VII, Pope may optionally be commemorated only in the Daily Office by adding the DWM 740 Collect after the Collect of the Day.

St Mary Magdalene de' Pazzi, Virgin may optionally be commemorated only in the Daily Office by adding the DWM 740 Collect after the Collect of the Day.

¶ Whitsun Week (being the Octave of Pentecost), with the special form of the *Communicantes* in the Roman Canon, ends with the Saturday morning Mass, before the celebration of Trinity Sunday (cf. DWM 485).

MP Pss: 137, 144   Lessons: Nm 27:15-end ♦ Mt   Te Deum
9:35-10:20

EP 1 of TRINITY SUNDAY

Pss: 104   Lessons: Is 61 ♦ 2 Tm 1:3-14

> ¶ *Salve Regina* may be said after EP or Compline from First Evensong of Trinity Sunday to the Eve of Advent Sunday.

26 SUN   TRINITY SUNDAY *Solemnity* (OT 8)   White
DWM 488 Gloria, Creed
Lec 165: Dt 4:32-34, 39-40 ♦ Ps 33:3-6, 9, 12, 17-18, 19, 21 ♦ Rom 8:14-17 ♦ Mt 28:16-20

MP Pss: 146-147   Lessons: Is 6:1-8 ♦ Mk 1:1-13   Te Deum
EP 2   111-113   Is 40:12-end ♦ 1 Pt 1:3-12

27 Mon   Feria   Green
Or:
St Augustine of Canterbury, Bishop   *White*
Memorial Day [US]   *Black/Violet*
DWM 488
Lec 347: 1 Pt 1:3-9 ♦ Mk 10:17-27
  Or, for St Augustine of Canterbury, Bishop: DWM 742
Lec 571: 1 Thes 2:2b-8 (#722.10) ♦ Mt 9:35-38 (#724.1)
  Or, for Memorial Day [US]: DWM 1022
Lec 668 or 1011-1016: any appropriate readings from The Commemoration of all the Faithful Departed or from the Masses for the Dead

> ¶ On the norms to be observed in celebrating Masses for the Dead, see the Rubrical Directory, no. 45 (DWM 130).

MP Pss: 1-3   Lessons: 1 Sm 1 ♦ Jas 1
EP   4, 7   1 Sm 2:1-21 ♦ Mk 1:14-31

28 Tue   Feria   Green
DWM 488
Lec 348: 1 Pt 1:10-16 ♦ Mk 10:28-31

MP Pss: 5-6   Lessons: 1 Sm 2:22-end ♦ Jas 2:1-13
EP   10-11   1 Sm 3 ♦ Mk 1:32-end

29 Wed   Feria   Green
Or:
St Paul VI, Pope   *White*
DWM 488

Lec 349: 1 Pt 1:18-25 ♦ Mk 10:32-45

    Or, for St Paul VI, Pope: DWM 927

MP	Pss: 119:I-III	Lessons:	1 Sm 4 ♦ Jas 2:14-end
EP	12-14		1 Sm 7 ♦ Mk 2:1-22

30 Thu   Feria   Green

DWM 488

Lec 350: 1 Pt 2:2-5, 9-12 ♦ Mk 10:46-52

MP	Pss: 18:I	Lessons:	1 Sm 8 ♦ Jas 3
EP	18:II		1 Sm 9:1-25 ♦ Mk 2:23-3:12

31 Fri   Visitation of the Blessed Virgin Mary *Feast*   White

DWM 744 Gloria

Lec 572: Zep 3:14-18a or Rom 12:9-16b ♦ Ecce Deus, DWDO 74 ♦ Lk 1:39-56

MP	Pss: 72	Lessons:	1 Sm 2:1-10 ♦ Mk 3:31-35 Te Deum
EP	146-147 or 132		Nm 11:16-17, 24-29 or Sg 2:8-14 ♦ Lk 1:5-25

June 2024

1 Sat   Saint Justin, Martyr *Memorial*   Red
DWM 748
Lec 352: Jude 17, 20b-25 ♦ Mk 11:27-33
    Or:
Lec 574: 1 Cor 1:18-25 (#722.2) ♦ Mt 5:13-19 (#730.1)

MP Pss: 20-21   Lessons: 1 Sm 11 ♦ Jas 5
EP 1 of Corpus Christi
        Pss: 145   Lessons: Ex 16:14-18 ♦ Mk 14:22-24

2 SUN   MOST HOLY BODY AND BLOOD OF CHRIST *Solemnity*   White
DWM 552 Gloria, Creed
Lec 168: Ex 24:3-8 ♦ Ps 116:11-16 ♦ Heb 9:11-15 ♦ Mk 14:12-16, 22-26

> ¶ "The Sequence *Lauda Sion Salvatorem* may be sung or said" after the Alleluia verse (DWM 553).
>
> ¶ "It is desirable that a procession of the Most Blessed Sacrament take place after the Mass in which the Host to be carried in the procession is consecrated. However, nothing prohibits a procession from taking place even after a public and lengthy period of adoration following the Mass. If a procession takes place after Mass, when the Communion of the faithful is over, the monstrance in which the consecrated Host has been placed is set on the altar. When the Thanksgiving and the Postcommunion have been said, the concluding rites are omitted and the procession forms" (DWM 555).
>
> ❖ By decision of the Governing Council, ratified by the Bishop, the Solemnity of the Most Holy Body and Blood of Christ shall be celebrated on the first Sunday after Trinity, in keeping with the Latin Rite dioceses of the United States and Canada.

MP Pss: 78:1-8,19-30   Lessons: Gn 14:18-20 ♦ 1 Cor   Te Deum
                                               11:23-26
EP 2   23, 34:1-10   Prv 9:1-6 ♦ Mt 22:1-14

3 Mon   Saint Charles Lwanga and Companions, Martyrs *Memorial*   Red
DWM 750
Lec 353: 2 Pt 1:2-7 ♦ Mk 12:1-12
    Or:
Lec 576: 2 Mc 7:1-2, 9-14 (#713.3) ♦ Mt 5:1-12a (#742.1)

MP Pss: 25   Lessons: 1 Sm 13 ♦ 1 Pt 1:1-21
EP   9, 15   1 Sm 14:1-23 ♦ Mk 4:35-5:20

4 Tue   Feria (of Trinity 1) (OT 9)   Green
DWM 490
Lec 354: 2 Pt 3:12-15a, 17-18 ♦ Mk 12:13-17

MP Pss: 26, 28   Lessons: 1 Sm 14:24-48 ♦ 1 Pt 1:22-2:10
EP   36, 39   1 Sm 15 ♦ Mk 5:21-end

5 Wed   Saint Boniface, Bishop and Martyr *Memorial*   Red
DWM 750
Lec 355: 2 Tm 1:1-3, 6-12 ♦ Mk 12:18-27
    Or:
Lec 577: Acts 26:19-23 (#720.3) ♦ Jn 10:11-16 (#724.10)

MP Pss: 38   Lessons: 1 Sm 16 ♦ 1 Pt 2:11-3:7
EP   119:IV-VI   1 Sm 17:1-30 ♦ Mk 6:1-29

6 Thu   Feria   Green
            Or:
            St Norbert, Bishop   *White*
DWM 490
Lec 356: 2 Tm 2:8-15 ♦ Mk 12:28b-34
    Or, for St Norbert, Bishop: DWM 752
Lec 578: Ez 34:11-16 (#719.9) ♦ Lk 14:25-33 (#742.23)

MP Pss: 37:I   Lessons: 1 Sm 17:31-54 ♦ 1 Pt 3:8-4:6
EP 1 of THE MOST SACRED HEART OF JESUS
      Pss: 25   Lessons: Hos 11:1-9 ♦ Jn 19:31-37

7 Fri   MOST SACRED HEART OF JESUS *Solemnity*   White
DWM 556 Gloria, Creed
Lec 171: Hos 11:1, 3-4, 8c-9 ♦ Ecce Deus (DWDO 74) ♦ Eph 3:8-12, 14-19 ♦ Jn 19:31-37

MP Pss: 33   Lessons: Jer 31:31-34 ♦ Eph 2:4-10   Te Deum
EP 2   34   Is 12 ♦ Jn 7:37-39

> ¶ Today being a *Solemnity,* the obligation to abstain from meat or to perform some other penitential act is dispensed (CIC 1251).

8 Sat   The Immaculate Heart of the Blessed Virgin Mary *Memorial*   White
DWM 746
Lec 358: 2 Tm 4:1-8 ♦ Mk 12:38-44
    Or:
Lec 573: Is 61:9-11 (#707.9) ♦ **Lk 2:41-51**

MP Pss: 30, 32   Lessons: 1 Sm 20:18-end ♦ 1 Pt 5
EP 1 of The Second Sunday after Trinity
      Pss: 42-43   Lessons: 1 Sm 21:1-22:5 ♦ Mk 7:24-8:10

9 SUN   SECOND SUNDAY AFTER TRINITY (OT 10)   Green
DWM 492 Gloria, Creed
Lec 89: Gn 3:9-15 ♦ Ps 130:1-8 ♦ 2 Cor 4:13-5:1 ♦ Mk 3:20-35

MP Pss: 63, 98   Lessons: Jer 7:1-16 ♦ Acts 13:1-13   Te Deum
                                   (14-26)
EP 2   103   1 Kgs 8:22-30 (9:1-3) ♦ Jn 13:21-end

10 Mon   Feria   Green
DWM 492
Lec 359: 1 Kgs 17:1-6 ♦ Mt 5:1-12

MP Pss: 41, 52   Lessons: 1 Sm 22:6-end ♦ 2 Pt 1
EP   44   1 Sm 23 ♦ Mk 8:11-9:1

11 Tue   Saint Barnabas, Apostle *Memorial*   Red
DWM 753
Lec 360: 1 Kgs 17:7-16 ♦ Mt 5:13-16
      Or:
Lec 580: **Acts 11:21b-26; 13:1-3** ♦ Ps 98:1-7 ♦ Mt 10:7-13

MP Pss: 45   Lessons: 1 Sm 24 ♦ 2 Pt 2
EP   47-48   1 Sm 25:2-42 ♦ Mk 9:2-29

12 Wed   Feria   Green
DWM 492
Lec 361: 1 Kgs 18:20-39 ♦ Mt 5:17-19

MP Pss: 119:VII-IX   Lessons: 1 Sm 26 ♦ 2 Pt 3
EP   49, 53   1 Sm 28:3-end ♦ Mk 9:30-end

13 Thu   Saint Anthony of Padua, Priest and Doctor of the Church *Memorial*   White
DWM 755
Lec 362: 1 Kgs 18:41-46 ♦ Mt 5:20-26
      Or:
Lec 581: Is 61:1-3abcd (#719.6) ♦ Lk 10:1-9 (#724.8)

MP Pss: 50   Lessons: 1 Sm 31 ♦ Jude
EP   59-60 or 8, 84   2 Sm 1 ♦ Mk 10:1-31

14 Fri   Feria   Green
DWM 492
Lec 363: 1 Kgs 19:9a, 11-16 ♦ Mt 5:27-32

MP Pss: 40, 54   Lessons: 2 Sm 2:1-3:1 ♦ 1 Jn 1:1-2:6
EP   51   2 Sm 3:17-end ♦ Mk 10:32-end

15 Sat   Feria   Green
             Or:
             BVM: Mass of Saint Mary 5   *White*
DWM 492
Lec 364: 1 Kgs 19:19-21 ♦ Mt 5:33-37
             Or, for Saint Mary: DWM 996
Lec 707-712 any readings from the Common of the BVM

MP Pss: 55   Lessons: 2 Sm 5:1-12 ♦ 1 Jn 2:7-end
EP 1 of The Third Sunday after Trinity
     Pss: 138-139   Lessons: 2 Sm 6 ♦ Mk 11:1-26

16 SUN   THIRD SUNDAY AFTER TRINITY (OT 11)   Green
DWM 494 Gloria, Creed
Lec 92: Ez 17:22-24 ♦ Ps 92:1-2, 11-14 ♦ 2 Cor 5:6-10 ♦ Mk 4:26-34

MP Pss: 24, 29   Lessons: Jer 17:5-14 ♦ Acts 16:6-34   Te Deum
EP 2   8, 84   1 Kgs 10:1-13 ♦ Jn 14:1-14

17 Mon   Feria   Green
DWM 494
Lec 365: 1 Kgs 21:1-16 ♦ Mt 5:38-42

MP Pss: 56-58   Lessons: 2 Sm 7 ♦ 1 Jn 3:1-12
EP   64-65   2 Sm 9 ♦ Mk 11:27-12:12

18 Tue   Feria   Green
DWM 494
Lec 366: 1 Kgs 21:17-29 ♦ Mt 5:43-48

MP Pss: 61-62   Lessons: 2 Sm 11 ♦ 1 Jn 3:13-4:6
EP   68   2 Sm 12:1-23 ♦ Mk 12:13-34

June 2024

19 Wed   Feria   Green
               Or:
               St Romuald, Abbot   *White*
               DWM 494
               Lec 367: 2 Kgs 2:1, 6-14 ♦ Mt 6:1-6, 16-18
                   Or, for St Romuald, Abbot: DWM 756
               Lec 582: Phil 3:8-14 (#740.9) ♦ Lk 14:25-33 (#742.23)

               MP Pss: 72   Lessons: 2 Sm 13:38-14:24 ♦ 1 Jn 4:7-end
               EP   119:X-XII   2 Sm 14:25-15:12 ♦ Mk 12:35-13:13

20 Thu   Feria   Green
               Or:
               St Alban, Protomartyr of England   *Red*
               DWM 494
               Lec 368: Sir 48:1-14 ♦ Mt 6:7-15
                   Or, for St Alban, Protomartyr of England: DWM 756

               MP Pss: 70-71   Lessons: 2 Sm 15:13-end ♦ 1 Jn 5
               EP   74   2 Sm 16:1-19 ♦ Mk 13:14-end

21 Fri   Saint Aloysius Gonzaga, Religious *Memorial*   White
               DWM 758
               Lec 369: 2 Kgs 11:1-4, 9-18, 20 ♦ Mt 6:19-23
                   Or:
               Lec 583: 1 Jn 5:1-5 (#740.18) ♦ Mt 22:34-40 (#742.10)

               MP Pss: 69   Lessons: 2 Sm 17:1-23 ♦ 2 Jn
               EP   73   2 Sm 17:24-18:18 ♦ Mk 14:1-26

22 Sat   Saints John Fisher, Bishop, and Thomas More, Martyrs *Memorial*   Red
               DWM 759
               Lec 370: 2 Chr 24:17-25 ♦ Mt 6:24-34
                   Or:
               Lec 585: 1 Pt 4:12-19 (#716.9) ♦ Mt 10:34-39 (#718.3)

               MP Pss: 75-76   Lessons: 2 Sm 18:19-end ♦ 3 Jn
               EP 1 of The Fourth Sunday after Trinity
                   Pss: 23, 27   Lessons: 2 Sm 19:1-23 ♦ Mk 14:27-52

June 2024

23 SUN   FOURTH SUNDAY AFTER TRINITY (OT 12)   Green
DWM 496 Gloria, Creed
Lec 95: Jb 38:1, 8-11 ♦ Ps 107:1, 23-26, 28-31 ♦ 2 Cor 5:14-17 ♦ Mk 4:35-41

MP Pss: 93, 96   Lessons: Jer 18:1-17 ♦ Acts   Te Deum
                                       17:16-end
EP 1 of THE NATIVITY OF ST JOHN THE BAPTIST
       Pss: 103   Lessons: Mal 3:1-6 ♦ Lk 3:1-20

24 Mon   NATIVITY OF SAINT JOHN THE BAPTIST *Solemnity*   White
<u>Vigil</u>
DWM 763 Gloria, Creed
Lec 586: Jer 1:4-10 ♦ Ps 71:1-5, 14, 16 ♦ 1 Pt 1:8-12 ♦ Lk 1:5-17
<u>Day</u>
DWM 764 Gloria, Creed
Lec 587: Is 49:1-6 ♦ Ps 139:1-2, 12-14 ♦ Acts 13:22-26 ♦ Lk 1:57-66, 80

MP Pss: 82, 98   Lessons: Jgs 13:1-7 ♦ Lk 1:5-25   Te Deum
EP 2   80   Mal 4 ♦ Mt 11:2-19

25 Tue   Feria   Green
DWM 496
Lec 372: 2 Kgs 19:9b-11, 14-21, 31-35a, 36 ♦ Mt 7:6, 12-14

MP Pss: 78:I   Lessons: 2 Sm 24 ♦ Rom 2:1-16
EP   78:II   1 Kgs 1:5-31 ♦ Mk 15:1-41

26 Wed   Feria   Green
DWM 496
Lec 373: 2 Kgs 22:8-13; 23:1-3 ♦ Mt 7:15-20

MP Pss: 119:XIII-XV   Lessons: 1 Kgs 1:32-end ♦ Rom 2:17-end
EP   81-82   1 Chr 22:2-end ♦ Mk 15:42-16:end

27 Thu   Feria   Green
              Or:
              St Cyril of Alexandria, Bishop and Doctor of the Church   *White*
              Can: *Bls Nykyta Budka and Vasyl Velychkowsky, Bishops and Martyrs*   *Red*
DWM 496
Lec 374: 2 Kgs 24:8-17 ♦ Mt 7:21-29
       Or, for St Cyril of Alexandria, Bishop and Doctor of the Church: DWM 766
Lec 588: 2 Tm 4:1-5 (#722.12) ♦ Mt 5:13-19 (#730.1)

June 2024

Or, for Bls Nykyta Budka and Vasyl Velychkowsky, Bishops and Martyrs: DWM 917

| MP | Pss: 83 | Lessons: 1 Chr 28:1-10 ♦ Rom 3 |
| EP | 85-86 | 1 Chr 28:20-29:9 ♦ Lk 1:1-23 |

28 Fri   Saint Irenaeus, Bishop and Martyr *Memorial*   Red
DWM 766
Lec 375: 2 Kgs 25:1-12 ♦ Mt 8:1-4
   Or:
Lec 589: 2 Tm 2:22b-26 ♦ Jn 17:20-26 (#742.26)

| MP | Pss: 88 | Lessons: 1 Chr 29:10-end ♦ Rom 4 |

EP 1 of STS PETER AND PAUL

| | Pss: 62-63 | Lessons: Ez 3:4-11 ♦ Gal 1:13-2:10 |

29 Sat   SAINTS PETER AND PAUL, APOSTLES *Solemnity*   Red
<u>Vigil</u>
DWM 767 Gloria, Creed
Lec 590: Acts 3:1-10 ♦ Ps 19:1-4 ♦ Gal 1:11-20 ♦ Jn 21:15-19
<u>Day</u>
DWM 769 Gloria, Creed
Lec 591: Acts 12:1-11 ♦ Ps 34:1-8 ♦ 2 Tm 4:6-8, 17-18 ♦ Mt 16:13-19

| MP | Pss: 66 | Lessons: Ez 2:1-7 ♦ Acts 11:1-18 | Te Deum |
| EP 2 | 97, 138 | Ez 34:11-16 ♦ Jn 21:15-22 | |

30 SUN   FIFTH SUNDAY AFTER TRINITY (OT 13)   Green
DWM 498 Gloria, Creed
Lec 98: Wis 1:13-15; 2:23-24 ♦ Ps 30:1, 3-5, 11-13 ♦ 2 Cor 8:7, 9, 13-15 ♦ Mk 5:21-43 or 5:21-24, 35-43

| MP | Pss: 66-67 | Lessons: Jer 26:1-16 ♦ Acts 19:21-end | Te Deum |
| EP | 19, 46 | 1 Kgs 18:17-39 ♦ Jn 15:1-16 | |

July 2024

1 Mon   Feria   Green
              Or:
              USA: *St Junipero Serra, Priest*   *White*
              Can: *Canada Day [Canada]*   *White*
              DWM 498
              Lec 377: Am 2:6-10, 13-16 ♦ Mt 8:18-22
                   Or, for St Junipero Serra, Priest: DWM 771
                   Or, for Canada Day [Canada]: DWM 1015
              Lec 882-886 or 887-891: any readings from the Mass For the Country or a City, or For Peace and Justice

              MP   Pss: 89:I   Lessons: 1 Kgs 6:1-14 ♦ Rom 6
              EP   89:II   1 Kgs 8:1-21 ♦ Lk 2:1-21

2 Tue   Feria   Green
              DWM 498
              Lec 378: Am 3:1-8; 4:11-12 ♦ Mt 8:23-27

              MP   Pss: 97, 99-100   Lessons: 1 Kgs 8:22-53 ♦ Rom 7
              EP   94-(95)   1 Kgs 8:54-9:9 ♦ Lk 2:22-end

3 Wed   Saint Thomas, Apostle *Feast*   Red
              DWM 772 Gloria
              Lec 593: Eph 2:19-22 ♦ Ps 117:1-2 ♦ Jn 20:24-29

              MP   Pss: 23, 121   Lessons: Jb 42:1-6 ♦ Jn 14:1-7   Te Deum
              EP   27   Gn 12:1-5a ♦ 1 Pt 1:3-9

4 Thu   Feria   Green
              Or:
              USA: *Independence Day [US]*   *White*
              Can: *St Elizabeth of Portugal*   *White*
              DWM 498
              Lec 380: Am 7:10-17 ♦ Mt 9:1-8
                   Or, for Independence Day [US]: DWM 1015
              Lec 882-886 or 887-891: any readings from the Mass For the Country or a City, or For Peace and Justice
                   Or, for St Elizabeth of Portugal: DWM 773
              Lec 594: 1 Jn 3:14-18 (#740.16) ♦ Mt 25:31-46 or 25:31-40 (#742.13)

MP Pss: 105:I   Lessons: 1 Kgs 11:26-end ♦ Rom 8:18-end
EP   105:II   1 Kgs 12:1-24 ♦ Lk 4:1-30

5 Fri   Feria   Green
             Or:
             St Anthony Zaccaria, Priest   *White*
             USA: *St Elizabeth of Portugal*   *White*
             DWM 498
             Lec 381: Am 8:4-6, 9-12 ♦ Mt 9:9-13
                 Or, for St Anthony Zaccaria, Priest: DWM 774
             Lec 595: 2 Tm 1:13-14; 2:1-3 (#722.11) ♦ Mk 10:13-16 (#742.16)
                 Or, for St Elizabeth of Portugal: DWM 773
             Lec 594: 1 Jn 3:14-18 (#740.16) ♦ Mt 25:31-46 or 25:31-40 (#742.13)

MP Pss: 102   Lessons: 1 Kgs 12:25-13:10 ♦ Rom 9
EP   107:I   1 Kgs 13:11-end ♦ Lk 4:31-end

6 Sat   Feria   Green
             Or:
             St Maria Goretti, Virgin and Martyr   *Red*
             BVM: Mass of Saint Mary 5   *White*
             DWM 498
             Lec 382: Am 9:11-15 ♦ Mt 9:14-17
                 Or, for St Maria Goretti, Virgin and Martyr: DWM 774
             Lec 596: 1 Cor 6:13c-15a, 17-20 ♦ Jn 12:24-26 (#718.5)
                 Or, for Saint Mary: DWM 996
             Lec 707-712 any readings from the Common of the BVM

MP Pss: 107:II, 108   Lessons: 1 Kgs 14:1-20 ♦ Rom 10
EP 1 of The Sixth Sunday after Trinity
        Pss: 33   Lessons: 2 Chr 12 ♦ Lk 5:1-16

7 SUN   SIXTH SUNDAY AFTER TRINITY (OT 14)   Green
             DWM 500 Gloria, Creed
             Lec 101: Ez 2:2-5 ♦ Ps 123:1-4 ♦ 2 Cor 12:7-10 ♦ Mk 6:1-6

MP Pss: 118   Lessons: Jer 30:1-3,10-22 ♦ Acts   Te Deum
                                  20:17-end
EP 2   145   1 Kgs 19:1-18 ♦ Jn 15:17-end

8 Mon   Feria   Green
DWM 500
Lec 383: Hos 2:14bc, 15cd-16, 19-20 ♦ Mt 9:18-26

MP Pss: 106:I   Lessons: 2 Chr 13 ♦ Rom 11:1-24
EP   106:II   2 Chr 14 ♦ Lk 5:17-end

9 Tue   Feria   Green
Or:
St Augustine Zhao Rong, Priest, and Companions, Martyrs   *Red*
Our Lady of the Atonement   *White*
DWM 500
Lec 384: Hos 8:4-7, 11-13 ♦ Mt 9:32-38
    Or, for St Augustine Zhao Rong, Priest, and Companions, Martyrs: DWM 775
    Or, for Our Lady of the Atonement: DWM 776
Lec 707-712 any reading from the Common of the Blessed Virgin Mary

MP Pss: 120-123   Lessons: 2 Chr 15 ♦ Rom 11:25-end
EP   124-127   2 Chr 16 ♦ Lk 6:1-19

10 Wed   Feria   Green
DWM 500
Lec 385: Hos 10:1-3, 7-8, 12 ♦ Mt 10:1-7

MP Pss: 119:XIX-XXII   Lessons: 1 Kgs 16:15-end ♦ Rom 12
EP   128-130   1 Kgs 17 ♦ Lk 6:20-38

11 Thu   Saint Benedict, Abbot *Memorial*   White
DWM 776
Lec 386: Hos 11:1-4, 8c-9 ♦ Mt 10:7-15
    Or:
Lec 597: Prv 2:1-9 ♦ Mt 19:27-29 (#742.9)

MP Pss: 131-133   Lessons: 1 Kgs 18:1-16 ♦ Rom 13
EP   134-135   1 Kgs 18:17-end ♦ Lk 6:39-7:10

12 Fri   Feria   Green
DWM 500
Lec 387: Hos 14:1-9 ♦ Mt 10:16-23

MP Pss: 140, 142   Lessons: 1 Kgs 19 ♦ Rom 14
EP   141, 143   1 Kgs 21 ♦ Lk 7:11-35

13 Sat	Feria	Green
	Or:	
	St Henry, Confessor	*White*
	BVM: Mass of Saint Mary 5	*White*

DWM 500

Lec 388: Is 6:1-8 ♦ Mt 10:24-33

    Or, for St Henry, Confessor: DWM 778

Lec 598: Mi 6:6-8 (#737.17) ♦ Mt 7:21-27 (#742.3)

    Or, for Saint Mary: DWM 996

Lec 707-712 any readings from the Common of the BVM

MP   Pss: 137, 144   Lessons: 1 Kgs 22:1-40 ♦ Rom 15:1-13

EP 1 of The Seventh Sunday after Trinity

        Pss: 104   Lessons: 2 Chr 20:1-30 ♦ Lk 7:36-end

14 SUN	SEVENTH SUNDAY AFTER TRINITY (OT 15)	Green

DWM 502 Gloria, Creed

Lec 104: Am 7:12-15 ♦ Ps 85:7-13 ♦ Eph 1:3-14 or 1:3-10 ♦ Mk 6:7-13

MP   Pss: 146-147   Lessons: Jer 31:27-34 ♦ Acts   Te Deum

                                            21:15-36

EP 2   111-113   1 Kgs 21:1-23(24-end) ♦ Jn 16:1-15

15 Mon	Saint Bonaventure, Bishop and Doctor of the Church *Memorial*	White

DWM 780

Lec 389: Is 1:10-17 ♦ Mt 10:34-11:1

    Or:

Lec 600: Eph 3:14-19 (#740.7) ♦ Mt 23:8-12 (#724.3)

MP   Pss: 1-3   Lessons: 2 Kgs 1 ♦ Rom 15:14-end

EP   4, 7   2 Kgs 2:1-22 ♦ Lk 8:1-21

16 Tue	Feria	Green
	Or:	
	Our Lady of Mount Carmel	*White*

DWM 502

Lec 390: Is 7:1-9 ♦ Mt 11:20-24

    Or, for Our Lady of Mount Carmel: DWM 781

Lec 601: Zec 2:10-13 (#707.11) ♦ Mt 12:46-50 (#712.3)

MP   Pss: 5-6   Lessons: 2 Kgs 4:1-37 ♦ Rom 16

EP   10-11   2 Kgs 5 ♦ Lk 8:22-end

17 Wed	Feria	Green

DWM 502

Lec 391: Is 10:5-7, 13-16 ♦ Mt 11:25-27

MP Pss: 119:I-III   Lessons: 2 Kgs 6:1-23 ♦ 1 Cor 1:1-25
EP   12-14   2 Kgs 6:24-7:2 ♦ Lk 9:1-17

18 Thu	Feria	Green

Or:

USA: *St Camillus de Lellis, Priest*   *White*

DWM 502

Lec 392: Is 26:7-9, 12, 16-19 ♦ Mt 11:28-30

     Or, for St Camillus de Lellis, Priest: DWM 779

Lec 599: 1 Jn 3:14-18 (#740.16) ♦ Jn 15:9-17 (#742.25)

MP Pss: 18:I   Lessons: 2 Kgs 7:3-end ♦ 1 Cor 1:26-2:end
EP   18:II   2 Kgs 8:1-15 ♦ Lk 9:18-50

19 Fri	Feria	Green

DWM 502

Lec 393: Is 38:1-6, 21-22, 7-8 ♦ Mt 12:1-8

MP Pss: 16-17   Lessons: 2 Kgs 9 ♦ 1 Cor 3
EP   22   2 Kgs 11:1-20 ♦ Lk 9:51-end

20 Sat	Feria	Green

Or:

St Apollinaris, Bishop and Martyr   *Red*
BVM: Mass of Saint Mary 5   *White*

DWM 502

Lec 394: Mi 2:1-5 ♦ Mt 12:14-21

     Or, for St Apollinaris, Bishop and Martyr: DWM 782
     Or, for Saint Mary: DWM 996

Lec 707-712 any readings from the Common of the BVM

MP Pss: 20-21   Lessons: 2 Kgs 11:21-12:end ♦ 1 Cor 4:1-17
EP 1 of The Eighth Sunday after Trinity
     Pss: 110, 116-117   Lessons: 2 Kgs 13 ♦ Lk 10:1-24

21 SUN	EIGHTH SUNDAY AFTER TRINITY (OT 16)	Green

DWM 504 Gloria, Creed

Lec 107: Jer 23:1-6 ♦ Ps 23:1-6 ♦ Eph 2:13-18 ♦ Mk 6:30-34

July 2024

MP	Pss: 148-150	Lessons:	Jer 36:1-26 ♦ Acts 25:1-12 Te Deum (13-end)
EP 2	114-115		1 Kgs 22:1-38 ♦ Jn 16:16-22

22 Mon   Saint Mary Magdalene *Feast*   White

DWM 783 Gloria

Lec 603: Sg 3:1-4ab or 2 Cor 5:14-17 ♦ Ps 63:1-6, 8-9 ♦ Jn 20:1-2, 11-18

> ¶ By decree of Pope Francis on 3 June 2016, the liturgical observance of St Mary Magdalene has been raised from a *Memorial* to a *Feast*. The *Gloria* shall be sung or said at all of her Masses on 22 July.

MP	Pss: 5-6	Lessons:	Is 25:1-9 ♦ Jn 20:1-10 Te Deum
EP	41-42 or 13, 16		Zep 3:14-end or 1 Sm 16:14-end ♦ Mk 15:40-end or Lk 8:1-3

23 Tue   Feria   Green

Or:

St Bridget of Sweden, Religious   *White*

DWM 504

Lec 396: Mi 7:14-15, 18-20 ♦ Mt 12:46-50

Or, for St Bridget of Sweden, Religious: DWM 785

Lec 604: Gal 2:19-20 (#740.5) ♦ Jn 15:1-8 (#742.24)

MP	Pss: 26, 28	Lessons:	2 Kgs 15:17-end ♦ 1 Cor 6
EP	36, 39		2 Kgs 16 ♦ Lk 11:1-28

24 Wed   Feria   Green

Or:

St Sharbel Makhluf, Priest   *White*

DWM 504

Lec 397: Jer 1:1, 4-10 ♦ Mt 13:1-9

Or, for St Sharbel Makhluf, Priest: DWM 786

MP	Pss: 38	Lessons:	Is 7:1-17 ♦ 1 Cor 7
EP	119:IV-VI		Is 8:1-18 ♦ Lk 11:29-end

25 Thu   Saint James, Apostle *Feast*   Red

DWM 787 Gloria

Lec 605: 2 Cor 4:7-15 ♦ Ps 126:1-7 ♦ Mt 20:20-28

MP	Pss: 34	Lessons:	Jer 26:1-15 ♦ Lk 9:46-56 Te Deum
EP	33		Jer 45 ♦ Mk 14:32-42

July 2024

26 Fri   Saints Joachim and Anne, Parents of the Blessed Virgin Mary *(USA:*   White
            Memorial, Can: Feast)
DWM (USA:) 788 (Can:) 788 Gloria
USA: Lec 399: Jer 3:14-17 ♦ Mt 13:18-23
    Or:
USA: Lec 606: Sir 44:1, 10-15 ♦ Ps 132:11-12, 14-15, 18-19 ♦ Mt 13:16-17
Can: Lec 606: Sir 44:1, 10-15 ♦ Ps 132:11-12, 14-15, 18-19 ♦ Mt 13:16-17

USA:
MP Pss: 31   Lessons: 2 Kgs 18:1-8 ♦ 1 Cor 9
EP   35   2 Chr 30 ♦ Lk 12:35-53
Can:
MP Pss: 19   Lessons: Ex 20:1-17 ♦ Mt 13:18-23   Te Deum
EP   36   Jer 2:1-3, 7-8, 12-13 ♦ Mt 13:10-17

27 Sat   Feria   Green
    Or:
BVM: Mass of Saint Mary 5   *White*
DWM 504
Lec 400: Jer 7:1-11 ♦ Mt 13:24-30
    Or, for Saint Mary: DWM 996
Lec 707-712 any readings from the Common of the BVM

MP Pss: 30, 32   Lessons: 2 Kgs 18:13-end ♦ 1 Cor 10:1-11:1
EP 1 of The Ninth Sunday after Trinity
       Pss: 42-43   Lessons: 2 Kgs 19 ♦ Lk 12:54-13:9

28 SUN   NINTH SUNDAY AFTER TRINITY (OT 17)   Green
DWM 506 Gloria, Creed
Lec 110: 2 Kgs 4:42-44 ♦ Ps 145:10-11, 15-18 ♦ Eph 4:1-6 ♦ Jn 6:1-15

MP Pss: 63, 98   Lessons: Jer 38:1-13 ♦ Acts 27   Te Deum
EP 2   103   2 Kgs 4:8-37 ♦ Jn 16:23-end

29 Mon   Sts Martha, Mary, and Lazarus *Memorial*   White
DWM 940
Lec 401: Jer 13:1-11 ♦ Mt 13:31-35
    Or:
Lec 607: 1 Jn 4:7-16 (#740.17) ♦ Jn 11:19-27 or Lk 10:38-42

¶ An interim Mass formulary has been approved by the USCCB for the Memorial of Saints Martha, Mary, and Lazarus for use at this time. It is presented according to DWM here. The Collect is taken from the Commons of Holy Men & Women (DWM 940); the Prayer over the Offerings and Postcommunion are adaptations of the Propers for St. Martha (DWM 790). The minor propers continue from the Common of Virgins, (DWM 938-939).

Collect

ALMIGHTY God, who willest to be glorified in thy Saints, and didst raise up thy servants Martha, Mary, and Lazarus to shine as lights in the world: shine we pray thee, in our hearts; that aided by their prayers we also in our generation may show forth thy praises, who hast called us out of darkness into thy marvellous light; through Jesus Christ thy Son our Lord, who liveth and reigneth with thee, in the unity of the Holy Spirit, ever one God, world without end. Amen.

Prayer over the Offerings

WE beseech thee, O Lord, as we proclaim thy wonders in thy saints: and humbly implore thy majesty; that, as their homage of love was pleasing unto thee, so our dutiful service may find favour in thy sight; through Jesus Christ our Lord. Amen.

Postcommunion

MAY the holy reception of the Body and Blood of thine Only Begotten Son, O Lord, turn us away from the cares of this fallen world: that, following the example of Saints Martha, Mary and Lazarus, we may grow in sincere love for thee on earth, and rejoice to behold thee for eternity in heaven; through Jesus Christ our Lord. Amen.

† The Rev. Msgr. Laurence Gipson, July 29, 2021

MP	Pss: 41, 52	Lessons: 2 Kgs 20 ♦ 1 Cor 11:2-end	
EP	44	2 Chr 33 ♦ Lk 13:10-end	

30 Tue   Feria   Green

Or:

St Peter Chrysologus, Bishop and Doctor of the Church   *White*

DWM 506

Lec 402: Jer 14:17b-22 ♦ Mt 13:36-43

    Or, for St Peter Chrysologus, Bishop and Doctor of the Church: DWM 790

Lec 608: Eph 3:8-12 (#728.4) ♦ Lk 6:43-45 (#730.6)

MP	Pss: 45	Lessons: 2 Kgs 22 ♦ 1 Cor 12:1-27	
EP	47-48	2 Kgs 23:1-20 ♦ Lk 14:1-24	

31 Wed   Saint Ignatius of Loyola, Priest *Memorial*   White

DWM 791

Lec 403: Jer 15:10, 16-21 ♦ Mt 13:44-46

Or:

Lec 609: 1 Cor 10:31-11:1 ♦ Lk 14:25-33 (#742.23)

MP Pss: 119:VII-IX   Lessons: 2 Kgs 23:21-35 ♦ 1 Cor 12:27-13:end
EP   49, 53   2 Kgs 23:36-24:17 ♦ Lk 14:25-15:10

August 2024

1 Thu   Saint Alphonsus Liguori, Bishop and Doctor of the Church *Memorial*   White
DWM 793
Lec 404: Jer 18:1-6 ♦ Mt 13:47-53
Or:
Lec 610: Rom 8:1-4 ♦ Mt 5:13-19 (#730.1)

MP Pss: 50   Lessons: 2 Kgs 24:18-25:7 ♦ 1 Cor 14:1-19
EP   59-60   2 Kgs 25:8-end ♦ Lk 15:11-end

2 Fri   Feria   Green
               Or:
               St Eusebius of Vercelli, Bishop   *White*
               St Peter Julian Eymard, Priest   *White*
DWM 506
Lec 405: Jer 26:1-9 ♦ Mt 13:54-58
      Or, for St Eusebius of Vercelli, Bishop: DWM 794
Lec 611: 1 Jn 5:1-5 (#716.10) ♦ Mt 5:1-12a (#742.1)
      Or, for St Peter Julian Eymard, Priest: DWM 794
Lec 611A: Acts 4:32-35 (#738.1) ♦ Jn 15:1-8 (#742.24)

MP Pss: 40, 54   Lessons: Jer 19 ♦ 1 Cor 14:20-end
EP   51   Jer 21:1-10 ♦ Lk 16

3 Sat   Feria   Green
               Or:
               BVM: Mass of Saint Mary 5   *White*
DWM 506
Lec 406: Jer 26:11-16, 24 ♦ Mt 14:1-12
      Or, for Saint Mary: DWM 996
Lec 707-712 any readings from the Common of the BVM

MP Pss: 55   Lessons: Jer 22:20-23:8 ♦ 1 Cor 15:1-34
EP 1 of The Tenth Sunday after Trinity
        Pss: 138-139   Lessons: Jer 24 ♦ Lk 17:1-19

4 SUN   TENTH SUNDAY AFTER TRINITY (OT 18)   Green
DWM 508 Gloria, Creed
Lec 113: Ex 16:2-4, 12-15 ♦ Ps 78:1-4, 24*-26, 55, *Skip "so". ♦ Eph 4:17, 20-24 ♦
Jn 6:24-35

August 2024

MP Pss: 24, 29   Lessons: Jer 52:1-11 ♦ Acts   Te Deum
                               28:11-end

EP 2   8, 84   2 Kgs 5:1-19 (20-end) ♦ Jn 17

---

5 Mon   Feria   Green

              Or:

              The Dedication of the Basilica of Saint Mary Major   *White*

              Can: *Bl Frédéric Janssoone, Priest*   *White*

              DWM 508

              Lec 407: Jer 28:1-17 ♦ Mt 14:13-21

                    Or, for The Dedication of the Basilica of Saint Mary Major: DWM 795

              Lec 613: Rv 21:1-5a (#708.3) ♦ Lk 11:27-28 (#712.10)

                    Or, for Bl Frédéric Janssoone, Priest: DWM 932

MP Pss: 56-58   Lessons: Jer 25:1-14 ♦ 1 Cor 15:35-end

EP   64-65   Jer 27:2-end ♦ Lk 17:20-end

---

6 Tue   Transfiguration of the Lord *Feast*   White

DWM 796 Gloria

Lec 614: Dn 7:9-10, 13-14 ♦ Ps 97:1-2, 5-6, 9 ♦ 2 Pt 1:16-19 ♦ Mk 9:2-10

MP Pss: 96-97   Lessons: Ex 34:29-end ♦ 2 Cor 3   Te Deum

EP   27, 93   Sir 48:1-16 ♦ 1 Jn 3:1-8

---

7 Wed   Feria   Green

              Or:

              St Sixtus II, Pope and Martyr, and Companions, Martyrs   *Red*

              St Cajetan, Priest   *White*

              DWM 508

              Lec 409: Jer 31:1-7 ♦ Mt 15:21-28

                    Or, for St Sixtus II, Pope and Martyr, and Companions, Martyrs: DWM 797

              Lec 615: Wis 3:1-9c (#713.5) ♦ Mt 10:28-33 (#718.2)

                    Or, for St Cajetan, Priest: DWM 798

              Lec 616: Sir 2:7-11 (#737.12) ♦ Lk 12:32-34 (#742.21)

MP Pss: 72   Lessons: Jer 32:1-25 ♦ 2 Cor 1:1-22

EP   119:X-XII   Jer 32:26-end ♦ Lk 18:31-19:10

---

8 Thu   Saint Dominic, Priest *Memorial*   White

DWM 798

Lec 410: Jer 31:31-34 ♦ Mt 16:13-23

            Or:

Lec 617: 1 Cor 2:1-10a (#728.2) ♦ Lk 9:57-62 (#742.19)

MP Pss: 70-71	Lessons: Jer 33 ♦ 2 Cor 1:23-2:end
EP 74	Jer 34:8-end ♦ Lk 19:11-28

9 Fri   Feria   Green

Or:

St Teresa Benedicta of the Cross (Edith Stein), Virgin and Martyr   *Red*

DWM 508

Lec 411: Na 1:15; 2:2; 3:1-3, 6-7 ♦ Mt 16:24-28

Or, for St Teresa Benedicta of the Cross (Edith Stein), Virgin and Martyr: DWM 801

MP Pss: 69	Lessons: Jer 37 ♦ 2 Cor 3
EP 73	Jer 38:1-13 ♦ Lk 19:29-end

10 Sat   Saint Lawrence, Deacon and Martyr *Feast*   Red

DWM 803 Gloria

Lec 618: 2 Cor 9:6b-10 ♦ Ps 112:1-2, 5-9 ♦ Jn 12:24-26

MP Pss: 31:1-20, 124	Lessons: 2 Mc 6:18-31 ♦ Acts 6:1-6, Te Deum
	8:1b, 4-8

EP 1 of The Eleventh Sunday after Trinity

         Pss: 23, 27   Lessons: Jer 39 ♦ Lk 20:1-26

11 SUN   ELEVENTH SUNDAY AFTER TRINITY (OT 19)   Green

DWM 510 Gloria, Creed

Lec 116: 1 Kgs 19:4-8 ♦ Ps 34:1-8 ♦ Eph 4:30-5:2 ♦ Jn 6:41-51

MP Pss: 93, 96	Lessons: Ez 11:14-20 ♦ Lk 4:1-15 Te Deum
EP 2 34	2 Kgs 17:1-23 ♦ Gal 1

12 Mon   Feria   Green

Or:

St Jane Frances de Chantal, Religious   *White*

DWM 510

Lec 413: Ez 1:2-5, 24-28c ♦ Mt 17:22-27

Or, for St Jane Frances de Chantal, Religious: DWM 805

Lec 691: Prv 31:10-13, 19-20, 30-31 (#737.11) ♦ Mk 3:31-35 (#742.14)

MP Pss: 80	Lessons: Jer 40 ♦ 2 Cor 5:1-19
EP 77, 79	Jer 41 ♦ Lk 20:27-21:4

13 Tue   Feria   Green

Or:

Sts Pontian, Pope, and Hippolytus, Priest, Martyrs   *Red*

DWM 510

Lec 414: Ez 2:8-3:4 ♦ Mt 18:1-5, 10, 12-14

    Or, for Sts Pontian, Pope, and Hippolytus, Priest, Martyrs: DWM 805

Lec 620: 1 Pt 4:12-19 (#716.9) ♦ Jn 15:18-21 (#718.6)

MP Pss: 78:I   Lessons: Jer 42 ♦ 2 Cor 5:20-7:1

EP   78:II   Jer 43 ♦ Lk 21:5-end

14 Wed   Saint Maximilian Mary Kolbe, Priest and Martyr *Memorial*   Red

DWM 806

Lec 415: Ez 9:1-7; 10:18-22 ♦ Mt 18:15-20

    Or:

Lec 620A: Wis 3:1-9c (#713.5), or 1 Jn 3:14-18 (#740.16) ♦ Jn 15:12-16

MP Pss: 119:XIII-XV   Lessons: Jer 44:1-14 ♦ 2 Cor 7:2-end

EP 1 of THE ASSUMPTION

        Pss: 110, 113, 122   Lessons: Prv 8:22-31 ♦ Jn 19:23-27

15 Thu   ASSUMPTION OF THE BLESSED VIRGIN MARY *Solemnity* HDO   White

<u>Vigil</u>

DWM 806 Gloria, Creed

Lec 621: 1 Chr 15:3-4, 15-16; 16:1-2 ♦ Ps 132:6-10, 14-15 ♦ 1 Cor 15:54b-57 ♦ Lk 11:27-28

<u>Day</u>

DWM 808 Gloria, Creed

Lec 622: Rv 11:19a; 12:1-6a, 10ab ♦ Ps 45:9-11, 15 ♦ 1 Cor 15:20-27 ♦ Lk 1:39-56

MP Pss: 85, 87, 97   Lessons: Is 7:10-15 ♦ Lk 11:27-28   Te Deum

EP 2   111, 127, 147   Sg 2:1-7 ♦ Acts 1:6-14

16 Fri   Feria   Green

Or:

St Stephen of Hungary   *White*

DWM 510

Lec 417: Ez 16:1-15, 60, 63 or 16:59-63 ♦ Mt 19:3-12

    Or, for St Stephen of Hungary: DWM 810

Lec 623: Dt 6:3-9 (#737.3) ♦ Mt 25:14-30 or 25:14-23 (#742.12)

MP Pss: 88   Lessons: Ez 3:4-end ♦ 2 Cor 9

EP   91-92   Ez 8 ♦ Lk 22:54-end

17 Sat	Feria	Green
	Or:	
	BVM: Mass of Saint Mary 5	*White*

DWM 510

Lec 418: Ez 18:1-10, 13b, 30-32 ♦ Mt 19:13-15

   Or, for Saint Mary: DWM 996

Lec 707-712 any readings from the Common of the BVM

MP Pss: 87, 90   Lessons: Ez 11:14-end ♦ 2 Cor 10

EP 1 of The Twelfth Sunday after Trinity

       Pss: 136   Lessons: Ez 12:17-end ♦ Lk 23:1-25

18 SUN	TWELFTH SUNDAY AFTER TRINITY (OT 20)	Green

DWM 512 Gloria, Creed

Lec 119: Prv 9:1-6 ♦ Ps 34:1-6, 8 ♦ Eph 5:15-20 ♦ Jn 6:51-58

MP Pss: 66-67   Lessons: Ez 18:1-4,19-end ♦ Lk   Te Deum

                                             4:16-30

EP 2   19, 46   2 Kgs 18:17-22, 18:28-19:7 ♦ Gal 6:1-10

19 Mon	Feria	Green
	Or:	
	St John Eudes, Priest	*White*

DWM 512

Lec 419: Ez 24:15-24 ♦ Mt 19:16-22

   Or, for St John Eudes, Priest: DWM 810

Lec 624: Eph 3:14-19 (#740.7) ♦ Mt 11:25-30 (#742.4)

MP Pss: 89:I   Lessons: Ez 13:1-16 ♦ 2 Cor 11

EP   89:II   Ez 14:1-11 ♦ Lk 23:26-49

20 Tue	Saint Bernard, Abbot and Doctor of the Church *Memorial*	White

DWM 811

Lec 420: Ez 28:1-10 ♦ Mt 19:23-30

   Or:

Lec 625: Sir 15:1-6 (#725.3) ♦ Jn 17:20-26 (#742.26)

MP Pss: 97, 99-100   Lessons: Ez 14:12-end ♦ 2 Cor 12:1-13

EP   94-(95)   Ez 20:1-20 ♦ Lk 23:50-24:12

21 Wed   Saint Pius X, Pope *Memorial*   White
DWM 812
Lec 421: Ez 34:1-11 ♦ Mt 20:1-16a
    Or:
Lec 626: 1 Thes 2:2b-8 (#722.10) ♦ Jn 21:15-17 (#724.12)

MP Pss: 101, 109   Lessons: Ez 20:27-44 ♦ 2 Cor 12:14-13:end
EP   119:XVI-XVIII   Ez 33:21-end ♦ Lk 24:13-end

22 Thu   The Queenship of the Blessed Virgin Mary *Memorial*   White
DWM 812
Lec 422: Ez 36:23-28 ♦ Mt 22:1-14
    Or:
Lec 627: Is 9:2-7 (#707.8) ♦ Lk 1:26-38 (#712.4)

MP Pss: 105:I   Lessons: Ez 34:1-16 ♦ Gal 1
EP   105:II   Ez 34:17-end ♦ Jn 1:1-28

23 Fri   Feria   Green
    Or:
    St Rose of Lima, Virgin   *White*
DWM 512
Lec 423: Ez 37:1-14 ♦ Mt 22:34-40
    Or, for St Rose of Lima, Virgin: DWM 814
Lec 628: 2 Cor 10:17-11:2 (#734.2) ♦ Mt 13:44-46 (#742.5)

MP Pss: 102   Lessons: Ez 36:22-36 ♦ Gal 2
EP   107:I   Ez 37:1-14 ♦ Jn 1:29-end

24 Sat   Saint Bartholomew, Apostle *Feast*   Red
DWM 814 Gloria
Lec 629: Rv 21:9b-14 ♦ Ps 145:10-13, 17-18 ♦ Jn 1:45-51

MP Pss: 86   Lessons: Dt 18:15-19 ♦ Mt 10:1-15   Te Deum
EP 1 of The Thirteenth Sunday after Trinity
    Pss: 33   Lessons: Ez 47:1-12 ♦ Jn 2

25 SUN   THIRTEENTH SUNDAY AFTER TRINITY (OT 21)   Green
DWM 514 Gloria, Creed
Lec 122: Jos 24:1-2a, 15-17, 18b ♦ Ps 34:1-2, 8, 15-20 ♦ Eph 5:21-32 or 5:2a, 25-32 ♦ Jn 6:60-69

August 2024

> ¶ The shorter version of today's 2nd reading in the citation above is not provided in the RSV-2CE lectionary. The shorter version inserts verse 5:2a ("Walk in love, as Christ loved us") in place of the text from "Be subject to one another" through "let wives also be subject in everything to their husbands."

MP Pss: 118	Lessons: Ez 33:1-11 ♦ Lk 6:20-38	Te Deum
EP 2 145	2 Kgs 19:8-35 ♦ 1 Cor 1:1-25	

26 Mon   Feria   Green
DWM 514
Lec 425: 2 Thes 1:1-5, 11b-12 ♦ Mt 23:13-22

MP Pss: 106:I	Lessons: Ezr 1 ♦ Gal 4:1-5:1
EP 106:II	Ezr 3 ♦ Jn 3:1-21

27 Tue   Saint Monica *Memorial*   White
DWM 818
Lec 426: 2 Thes 2:1-3a, 14-17 ♦ Mt 23:23-26
Or:
Lec 632: Sir 26:1-4, 13-16 (#737.14) ♦ Lk 7:11-17

MP Pss: 120-123	Lessons: Ezr 4 ♦ Gal 5:2-end
EP 124-127	Hg 1:1-2:9 ♦ Jn 3:22-end

28 Wed   Saint Augustine of Hippo, Bishop and Doctor of the Church *Memorial*   White
DWM 818
Lec 427: 2 Thes 3:6-10, 16-18 ♦ Mt 23:27-32
Or:
Lec 633: 1 Jn 4:7-16 (#740.17) ♦ Mt 23:8-12 (#730.4)

MP Pss: 119:XIX-XXII	Lessons: Zec 1:1-17 ♦ Gal 6
EP 128-130	Zec 1:18-2:end ♦ Jn 4:1-26

29 Thu   The Passion of Saint John the Baptist (*USA: Memorial, Can: Feast*)   Red
DWM (USA:) 819 (Can:) 819 Gloria
USA: Lec 428: 1 Cor 1:1-9 ♦ Mt 24:42-51
Or:
USA: Lec 634: Jer 1:17-19 ♦ Ps 71:1-5, 14, 16 ♦ **Mk 6:17-29**
Can: Lec 634: Jer 1:17-19 ♦ Ps 71:1-5, 14, 16 ♦ **Mk 6:17-29**

USA:

MP Pss: 131-133	Lessons: Zec 3 ♦ Eph 1:1-14
EP 134-135	Zec 4 ♦ Jn 4:27-end

Can:

MP Pss: 81, 82   Lessons: 2 Chr 24:17-22 ♦ Mt   Te Deum
                                    23:29-38
EP   119:XX-XXI   Lv 20:19-24 ♦ Mt 14:1-12

30 Fri   Feria   Green
              Or:
              Sts Margaret Clitherow, Anne Line, and Margaret Ward, Martyrs   *Red*
DWM 514
Lec 429: 1 Cor 1:17-25 ♦ Mt 25:1-13
       Or, for Sts Margaret Clitherow, Anne Line, and Margaret Ward, Martyrs: DWM
       820

MP Pss: 140, 142   Lessons: Zec 6:9-end ♦ Eph 1:15-end
EP   141, 143   Hg 2:10-end ♦ Jn 5:1-23

31 Sat   Feria   Green
              Or:
              St Aidan, Bishop, and the Saints of Lindisfarne   *White*
              BVM: Mass of Saint Mary 5   *White*
DWM 514
Lec 430: 1 Cor 1:26-31 ♦ Mt 25:14-30
       Or, for St Aidan, Bishop, and the Saints of Lindisfarne: DWM 821
       Or, for Saint Mary: DWM 996
Lec 707-712 any readings from the Common of the BVM

MP Pss: 137, 144   Lessons: Ezr 5 ♦ Eph 2:1-10
EP 1 of The Fourteenth Sunday after Trinity
       Pss: 104   Lessons: Ezr 6 ♦ Jn 5:24-end

September 2024

1 SUN FOURTEENTH SUNDAY AFTER TRINITY (OT 22)   Green
DWM 516 Gloria, Creed
Lec 125: Dt 4:1-2, 6-8 ♦ Ps 15:1-7 ♦ Jas 1:17-18, 21b-22, 27 ♦ Mk 7:1-8, 14-15, 21-23

MP	Pss: 146-147	Lessons:	Ez 33:21-end ♦ Lk 6:39-end	Te Deum
EP 2	111-113		2 Kgs 22 ♦ 1 Cor 1:26-2:9 (10-end)	

2 Mon Feria   Green
Or:
Labor Day
Can: *Bl André Grasset, Priest & Martyr*   *Red*
DWM 516
Lec 431: 1 Cor 2:1-5 ♦ Lk 4:16-30
  Or, for Labor Day: DWM 1013
Lec 907-911, any readings from the Mass for the Blessing of Human Labour
  Or, for Bl André Grasset, Priest & Martyr: DWM 919

MP	Pss: 1-3	Lessons:	Zec 7 ♦ Eph 2:11-end
EP	4, 7		Zec 8 ♦ Jn 6:1-21

3 Tue Saint Gregory the Great, Pope and Doctor of the Church *Memorial*   White
DWM 823
Lec 432: 1 Cor 2:10b-16 ♦ Lk 4:31-37
  Or:
Lec 635: 2 Cor 4:1-2, 5-7 (#722.6) ♦ Lk 22:24-30 (#724.9)

MP	Pss: 5-6	Lessons:	Ezr 7 ♦ Eph 3
EP	10-11		Ezr 8:15-end ♦ Jn 6:22-40

4 Wed Feria   Green
Or:
St Cuthbert, Bishop   *White*
Can: *Bl Dina Bélanger, Virgin*   *White*
DWM 516
Lec 433: 1 Cor 3:1-9 ♦ Lk 4:38-44
  Or, for St Cuthbert, Bishop: DWM 825
  Or, for Bl Dina Bélanger, Virgin: DWM 938

September 2024

MP Pss: 119:I-III	Lessons: Ezr 9 ♦ Eph 4:1-16	
EP 12-14	Ezr 10:1-19 ♦ Jn 6:41-end	

5 Thu Feria — Green
Or:
St Teresa of Calcutta, Virgin and Foundress — White
DWM 516
Lec 434: 1 Cor 3:18-23 ♦ Lk 5:1-11
Or, for St Teresa of Calcutta, Virgin and Foundress: DWM 938

MP Pss: 18:I Lessons: Neh 1 ♦ Eph 4:17-30
EP 18:II Neh 2 ♦ Jn 7:1-24

6 Fri Feria — Green
DWM 516
Lec 435: 1 Cor 4:1-5 ♦ Lk 5:33-39

MP Pss: 16-17 Lessons: Neh 4 ♦ Eph 4:31-5:21
EP 22 Neh 5 ♦ Jn 7:25-end

7 Sat Feria — Green
Or:
BVM: Mass of Saint Mary 5 — White
DWM 516
Lec 436: 1 Cor 4:6b-15 ♦ Lk 6:1-5
Or, for Saint Mary: DWM 996
Lec 707-712 any readings from the Common of the BVM

MP Pss: 20-21 Lessons: Neh 6:1-7:4 ♦ Eph 5:22-end
EP 1 of The Fifteenth Sunday after Trinity
Pss: 110, 116-117 Lessons: Neh 8 ♦ Jn 8:1-30

8 SUN FIFTEENTH SUNDAY AFTER TRINITY (OT 23) — Green
DWM 518 Gloria, Creed
Lec 128: Is 35:4-7a ♦ Ps 146:1, 4-10 ♦ Jas 2:1-5 ♦ Mk 7:31-37

> † The Rev. John Dale Cornelius, September 8, 2021.

MP Pss: 148-150 Lessons: Ez 34:1-16 ♦ Lk 7:36-8:3 Te Deum
EP 2 114-115 Ezr 1:1-8 ♦ 1 Cor 3

September 2024

9 Mon   Saint Peter Claver, Priest *Memorial*   White
DWM 827
Lec 437: 1 Cor 5:1-8 ♦ Lk 6:6-11

MP Pss: 25   Lessons: Neh 9:1-23 ♦ Eph 6:1-9
EP   9, 15   Neh 9:24-end ♦ Jn 8:31-end

10 Tue   Feria   Green
DWM 518
Lec 438: 1 Cor 6:1-11 ♦ Lk 6:12-19

MP Pss: 26, 28   Lessons: Neh 13 ♦ Eph 6:10-end
EP   36, 39   Dn 1 ♦ Jn 9

11 Wed   Feria   Green
DWM 518
Lec 439: 1 Cor 7:25-31 ♦ Lk 6:20-26

MP Pss: 38   Lessons: Dn 2:1-24 ♦ Phil 1:1-11
EP   119:IV-VI   Dn 2:25-end ♦ Jn 10:1-21

12 Thu   Feria   Green
           Or:
           The Most Holy Name of Mary   *White*
DWM 518
Lec 440: 1 Cor 8:1b-7, 11-13 ♦ Lk 6:27-38
           Or, for The Most Holy Name of Mary: DWM 827
Lec 707-712 any reading from the Common of the Blessed Virgin Mary

MP Pss: 37:I   Lessons: Dn 4:1-18 ♦ Phil 1:12-end
EP   37:II   Dn 4:19-end ♦ Jn 10:22-end

13 Fri   Saint John Chrysostom, Bishop and Doctor of the Church *Memorial*   White
DWM 828
Lec 441: 1 Cor 9:16-19, 22b-27 ♦ Lk 6:39-42
           Or:
Lec 637: Eph 4:1-7, 11-13 (#722.8) ♦ Mk 4:1-10, 13-20 or 4:1-9 (#730.5)

MP Pss: 31   Lessons: Dn 7:9-end ♦ Phil 2:1-11
EP   35   Dn 9 ♦ Jn 11:1-44

14 Sat   Exaltation of the Holy Cross *Feast*   Red

DWM 829 Gloria

Lec 638: Nm 21:4b-9 ♦ Ps 78:1-3, 8, 34-39 ♦ Phil 2:6-11 ♦ Jn 3:13-17

> ¶ Except on Sundays or when celebrated locally as a Solemnity of Title, there are only two readings. The OT reading is preferred as the first reading, but the rubrics allow the reading from Philippians to be used in its place. Sacristans and Readers should consult with the Celebrant or Homilist to ascertain the desired reading before setting the book and before reading.

MP Pss: 66   Lessons: Is 53 ♦ Phil 2:5-11   Te Deum

EP   118   Is 42:1-12 ♦ Eph 2:11-end

15 SUN   SIXTEENTH SUNDAY AFTER TRINITY (OT 24)   Green

DWM 520 Gloria, Creed

Lec 131: Is 50:5-9a ♦ Ps 116:1-9 ♦ Jas 2:14-18 ♦ Mk 8:27-35

MP Pss: 63, 98   Lessons: Ez 36:22-28,34-36 ♦ Lk   Te Deum

                                      9:46-end

EP   103   Ezr 3 ♦ 1 Cor 13

16 Mon   Saints Cornelius, Pope, and Cyprian, Bishop, Martyrs *Memorial*   Red

DWM 834

Lec 443: 1 Cor 11:17-26, 33 ♦ Lk 7:1-10

    Or:

Lec 640: 2 Cor 4:7-15 (#716.3) ♦ Jn 17:11b-19 (#718.7)

MP Pss: 41, 52   Lessons: Est 1 ♦ Phil 3

EP   44   Est 2:5-11,15-end ♦ Jn 12:1-19

17 Tue   Feria   Green

        Or:

        St Hildegard of Bingen, Virgin and Doctor of the Church   *White*

        St Robert Bellarmine, Bishop and Doctor of the Church   *White*

DWM 520

Lec 444: 1 Cor 12:12-14, 27-31a ♦ Lk 7:11-17

    Or, for St Hildegard of Bingen, Virgin and Doctor of the Church: DWM 938

    Or, for St Robert Bellarmine, Bishop and Doctor of the Church: DWM 835

Lec 641: Wis 7:7-10, 15-16 (#725.2) ♦ Mt 7:21-29 (#730.2)

MP Pss: 45   Lessons: Est 3 ♦ Phil 4

EP   47-48   Est 4 ♦ Jn 12:20-end

18 Wed	Ember Wednesday in September		Violet

DWM 524

Lec 445: 1 Cor 12:31-13:13 ♦ Lk 7:31-35

MP	Pss: 119:VII-IX	Lessons: Est 5 ♦ Col 1:1-20
EP	49, 53	Est 6 & 7 ♦ Jn 13

19 Thu	Feria		Green
	Or:		
	St Januarius, Bishop and Martyr		*Red*
	St Theodore of Canterbury, Bishop		*White*
	St Adrian, Abbot		*White*

DWM 520

Lec 446: 1 Cor 15:1-11 ♦ Lk 7:36-50

Or, for St Januarius, Bishop and Martyr: DWM 836

Lec 642: Heb 10:32-36 (#716.6) ♦ Jn 12:24-26 (#718.5)

Or, for St Theodore of Canterbury, Bishop: DWM 836

Or, for St Adrian, Abbot: DWM 945

MP	Pss: 50	Lessons: 1 Mc 1:1-19 ♦ Col 1:21-2:7
EP	59-60	1 Mc 1:20-40 ♦ Jn 14

20 Fri	Ember Friday in September, or		Violet
	St Andrew Kim Tae-gon, Priest, Paul Chong Ha-sang, and Companions, Martyrs *Memorial*		Red

DWM 526 or 837

Lec 447: 1 Cor 15:12-20 ♦ Lk 8:1-3

Or:

Lec 642A: Wis 3:1-9c (#713.5), or Rom 8:31b-39 (#716.2) ♦ Lk 9:23-26 (#718.4)

> ❖ On the recommendation of the Governing Council, the Bishop has decreed that Ember Friday in September is to be kept as an obligatory day of abstinence.

MP	Pss: 40, 54	Lessons: 1 Mc 1:41-end ♦ Col 2:8-19
EP	51	1 Mc 2:1-28 ♦ Jn 15

21 Sat	Saint Matthew, Apostle and Evangelist *Feast*		Red

DWM 838 Gloria

Lec 643: Eph 4:1-7, 11-13 ♦ Ps 19:1-4 ♦ Mt 9:9-13

MP	Pss: 37:I	Lessons: Prv 3:1-17 ♦ Mt 19:16-end	Te Deum

EP 1 of The Seventeenth Sunday after Trinity

	Pss: 138-139	Lessons: 1 Mc 2:49-end ♦ Jn 16

September 2024

> ❖ But at the Cathedral of Our Lady of Walsingham, for its *Solemnity of Title:*
> EP 1 of Our Lady of Walsingham
> Pss: 110, 113, 122 Lessons: Wis 9:1-12 ♦ Gal 4:1-5

22 SUN   SEVENTEENTH SUNDAY AFTER TRINITY (OT 25)   Green
DWM 522 Gloria, Creed
Lec 134: Wis 2:12, 17-20 ♦ Ps 54:1-4, 6 ♦ Jas 3:16-4:3 ♦ Mk 9:30-37

		Lessons:		
MP	Pss: 24, 29	Ez 37:15-end ♦ Lk 10:1-24	Te Deum	
EP 2	8, 84	Neh 1 ♦ Phil 1:12-end		

> ❖ But at the Cathedral of Our Lady of Walsingham, for its *Solemnity of Title,* replacing the texts for the Seventeenth Sunday after Trinity:
> DWM 840 Gloria, Creed
> Lec 707-712: readings from the Common of the BVM; or, as appointed in England & Wales, Gal 4:4-7 (no. 710-3) ♦ Jn 19:25b-27 (no. 712-12)
>
> | | | | Lessons: | | |
> |---|---|---|---|---|---|
> | MP | Pss: | 45-46, 87 | Is 52:7-12 ♦ Heb 2:5-end | Te Deum | |
> | EP 2 | | 111, 127, 147 or 110, 113, 122 | 1 Sm 2:1-10 or Wis 9:1-12 ♦ Mt 1:18-23 or Gal 4:1-5 | | |

23 Mon   Saint Pius of Pietrelcina, Priest *Memorial*   White
DWM 839
Lec 449: Prv 3:27-34 ♦ Lk 8:16-18
   Or:
Lec 643A: Gal 6:14-18 ♦ Mt 11:25-30 (#742.4)

		Lessons:	
MP	Pss: 56-58	1 Mc 3:1-26 ♦ Col 3:12-4:1	
EP	64-65	1 Mc 3:27-41 ♦ Jn 17	

24 Tue   Our Lady of Walsingham *Feast*   White
DWM 840 Gloria
Lec 707-712: readings from the Common of the BVM; or, as appointed in England & Wales, Gal 4:4-7 (no. 710-3) ♦ Jn 19:25b-27 (no. 712-12)

		Lessons:	
MP	Pss: 45-46, 87	Is 52:7-12 ♦ Heb 2:5-end	Te Deum
EP	111, 127, 147 or 110, 113, 122	1 Sm 2:1-10 or Wis 9:1-12 ♦ Mt 1:18-23 or Gal 4:1-5	

September 2024

> ❖ But at the Cathedral of Our Lady of Walsingham, its *Solemnity of Title* being celebrated on Sunday, 22 September:
>
> Feria (of Trinity 17, OT 25)
>
> DWM 522
>
> Lec 450: Prv 21:1-6, 10-13 ♦ Lk 8:19-21
>
> | MP | Pss: | 61-62 | Lessons: | 1 Mc 3:42-end ♦ Col 4:2-end |
> |---|---|---|---|---|
> | EP | | 68 | | 1 Mc 4:1-25 ♦ Jn 18:1-27 |

25 Wed   Feria   Green
Or:
Can: *Sts Cosmas and Damian, Martyrs*   *Red*
DWM 522
Lec 451: Prv 30:5-9 ♦ Lk 9:1-6
   Or, for Sts Cosmas and Damian, Martyrs: DWM 843
Lec 644: Wis 3:1-9c (#713.5) ♦ Mt 10:28-33 (#718.2)

MP	Pss: 72	Lessons:	1 Mc 4:26-35 ♦ Phlm
EP	119:X-XII		1 Mc 4:36-end ♦ Jn 18:28-end

26 Thu   USA: Feria   Green
Can: Saints Jean de Brébeuf and Isaac Jogues, Priests, and Companions,   Red
Martyrs *Feast*
Or:
USA: *Sts Cosmas and Damian, Martyrs*   *Red*
DWM (USA:) 522 (Can:) 862 Gloria
USA: Lec 452: Eccl 1:2-11 ♦ Lk 9:7-9
Can: Lec 662: 2 Cor 4:7-15 (#716.3) ♦ Mt 28:16-20 (#724.4)
   Or, for Sts Cosmas and Damian, Martyrs: DWM 843
Lec 644: Wis 3:1-9c (#713.5) ♦ Mt 10:28-33 (#718.2)

USA:

MP	Pss: 70-71	Lessons:	1 Mc 6:1-17 ♦ 1 Thes 1	
EP	74		1 Mc 6:18-47 ♦ Jn 19:1-30	

Can:

MP	Pss: 24, 63	Lessons:	2 Chr 24:18-22 ♦ 2 Cor 1:3-7	Te Deum
EP	16		2 Mc 6:18, 21, 24-31 ♦ 1 Pt 4:12-5:11	

27 Fri   Saint Vincent de Paul, Priest *Memorial*   White
DWM 844
Lec 453: Eccl 3:1-11 ♦ Lk 9:18-22
   Or:
Lec 645: 1 Cor 1:26-31 (#740.2) ♦ Mt 9:35-38 (#724.1)

MP Pss: 69   Lessons: 1 Mc 7:1-20 ♦ 1 Thes 2:1-16
EP   73   1 Mc 7:21-end ♦ Jn 19:31-end

28 Sat   Feria   Green
            Or:
            St Wenceslaus, Martyr   *Red*
            St Lawrence Ruiz and Companions, Martyrs   *Red*
            BVM: Mass of Saint Mary 5   *White*
            DWM 522
            Lec 454: Eccl 11:9-12:8 ♦ Lk 9:43b-45
                Or, for St Wenceslaus, Martyr: DWM 844
            Lec 646: 1 Pt 3:14-17 (#716.8) ♦ Mt 10:34-39 (#718.3)
                Or, for St Lawrence Ruiz and Companions, Martyrs: DWM 844
            Lec 646A: Job 3:1-3, 11-17, 20-23 ♦ Luke 9:51-56
                Or, for Saint Mary: DWM 996
            Lec 707-712 any readings from the Common of the BVM

            MP Pss: 75-76   Lessons: 1 Mc 9:1-22 ♦ 1 Thes 2:17-3:end
            EP 1 of The Eighteenth Sunday after Trinity
                Pss: 23, 27   Lessons: 1 Mc 13:41-end, 14:4-15 ♦ Jn 20

29 SUN   EIGHTEENTH SUNDAY AFTER TRINITY (OT 26)   Green
            DWM 530 Gloria, Creed
            Lec 137: Nm 11:25-29 ♦ Ps 19:7-9, 11-13 ♦ Jas 5:1-6 ♦ Mk 9:38-43, 45, 47-48

            MP Pss: 93, 96   Lessons: Dn 3 ♦ Lk 11:37-end   Te Deum
            EP 2   34   Neh 2 ♦ Phil 2:1-18

30 Mon   Saint Jerome, Priest and Doctor of the Church *Memorial*   White
            DWM 846
            Lec 455: Jb 1:6-22 ♦ Lk 9:46-50
                Or:
            Lec 648: 2 Tm 3:14-17 ♦ Mt 13:47-52 (#730.3)

            MP Pss: 80   Lessons: Jb 1 ♦ 1 Thes 4:1-12
            EP   77, 79   Jb 2 ♦ Jn 21

October 2024

1 Tue   Saint Thérèse of the Child Jesus, Virgin and Doctor of the Church *Memorial*   White
DWM 848
Lec 456: Jb 3:1-3, 11-17, 20-23 ♦ Lk 9:51-56
    Or:
Lec 649: Is 66:10-14c (#531) ♦ Mt 18:1-5 (#742.7)

MP	Pss: 78:I	Lessons:	Jb 3 ♦ 1 Thes 4:13-5:11
EP	78:II		Jb 4 ♦ Heb 1

2 Wed   Holy Guardian Angels *Memorial*   White
DWM 849
Lec 457: Jb 9:1-12, 14-16 ♦ Lk 9:57-62
    Or:
Lec 650: Ex 23:20-23 ♦ **Mt 18:1-5, 10**

MP	Pss: 119:XIII-XV	Lessons:	Jb 5 ♦ 1 Thes 5:12-end
EP	81-82		Jb 6 ♦ Heb 2

3 Thu   Feria   Green
DWM 530
Lec 458: Jb 19:21-27 ♦ Lk 10:1-12

> ✝ The Rev. Lowell Andrews, October 3, 2018

MP	Pss: 83	Lessons:	Jb 7 ♦ 2 Thes 1
EP	85-86		Jb 8 ♦ Heb 3

4 Fri   Saint Francis of Assisi *Memorial*   White
DWM 851
Lec 459: Jb 38:1, 12-21; 40:3-5 ♦ Lk 10:13-16
    Or:
Lec 651: Gal 6:14-18 ♦ Mt 11:25-30 (#742.4)

MP	Pss: 88	Lessons:	Jb 9 ♦ 2 Thes 2
EP	91-92		Jb 10 ♦ Heb 4:1-13

5 Sat   Feria   Green
      Or:
      St Faustina Kowalska, Virgin   *White*
      BVM: Mass of Saint Mary 5   *White*

USA: *Bl Francis Xavier Seelos, Priest*   *White*

DWM 530

Lec 460: Jb 42:1-3, 5-6, 12-17 ♦ Lk 10:17-24

    Or, for St Faustina Kowalska, Virgin: DWM 938

    Or, for Saint Mary: DWM 996

Lec 707-712 any readings from the Common of the BVM

    Or, for Bl Francis Xavier Seelos, Priest: DWM 944

MP Pss: 87, 90   Lessons: Jb 11 ♦ 2 Thes 3

EP 1 of The Nineteenth Sunday after Trinity

    Pss: 136   Lessons: Jb 12 ♦ Heb 4:14-5:10

6 SUN   NINETEENTH SUNDAY AFTER TRINITY (OT 27)   *Green*

DWM 532 Gloria, Creed

Lec 140: Gn 2:18-24 ♦ Ps 128:1-7 ♦ Heb 2:9-11 ♦ Mk 10:2-16 or 10:2-12

MP Pss: 66-67   Lessons: Dn 5 ♦ Lk 12:1-21   Te Deum

EP 2   19, 46   Ru 1 ♦ Phil 3:1-16

7 Mon   Our Lady of the Rosary *Memorial*   *White*

DWM 853

Lec 461: Gal 1:6-12 ♦ Lk 10:25-37

    Or:

Lec 653: Acts 1:12-14 (#708.1) ♦ Lk 1:26-38 (#712.4)

MP Pss: 89:I   Lessons: Jb 13 ♦ 1 Tm 1:1-17

EP   89:II   Jb 14 ♦ Heb 5:11-6:end

8 Tue   Feria   *Green*

    Or:

    St Denis, Bishop and Martyr, and Companions, Martyrs   *Red*

    St John Leonardi, Priest   *White*

DWM 532

Lec 462: Gal 1:13-24 ♦ Lk 10:38-42

    Or, for St Denis, Bishop and Martyr, and Companions, Martyrs: DWM 854

Lec 654: 2 Cor 6:4-10 (#716.4) ♦ Mt 5:13-16 (#742.2)

    Or, for St John Leonardi, Priest: DWM 855

Lec 655: 2 Cor 4:1-2, 5-7 (#722.6) ♦ Lk 5:1-11 (#724.7)

MP Pss: 97, 99-100   Lessons: Jb 15:1-16 ♦ 1 Tm 1:18-2:end

EP   94-(95)   Jb 16:1-17:2 ♦ Heb 7

9 Wed   Saint John Henry Newman, Priest *Memorial*   White

DWM 855

Lec 463: Gal 2:1-2, 7-14 ♦ Lk 11:1-4

> ❖ The Bishop has decreed that as a result of the canonization of Saint John Henry Newman, October 9th shall be kept as an Obligatory Memorial. When October 9th falls on a Sunday, the Memorial shall be transferred to Monday, October 10th.

MP Pss: 101, 109   Lessons: Jb 17:3-end ♦ 1 Tm 3
EP   119:XVI-XVIII   Jb 18 ♦ Heb 8

10 Thu   Feria   Green

DWM 532

Lec 464: Gal 3:1-5 ♦ Lk 11:5-13

MP Pss: 105:I   Lessons: Jb 19 ♦ 1 Tm 4
EP   105:II   Jb 21 ♦ Heb 9:1-14

11 Fri   Feria   Green
          Or:
          Saint John XXIII, Pope   *White*

DWM 532

Lec 465: Gal 3:7-14 ♦ Lk 11:15-26
    Or, for Saint John XXIII, Pope: DWM 856

MP Pss: 102   Lessons: Jb 22 ♦ 1 Tm 5
EP   107:I   Jb 23 ♦ Heb 9:15-end

12 Sat   Feria   Green
          Or:
          St Wilfrid, Bishop   *White*
          BVM: Mass of Saint Mary 5   *White*

DWM 532

Lec 466: Gal 3:22-29 ♦ Lk 11:27-28
    Or, for St Wilfrid, Bishop: DWM 857
    Or, for Saint Mary: DWM 996
Lec 707-712 any readings from the Common of the BVM

MP Pss: 107:II, 108   Lessons: Jb 24 ♦ 1 Tm 6
EP 1 of The Twentieth Sunday after Trinity
        Pss: 33   Lessons: Jb 25 & 26 ♦ Heb 10:1-18

October 2024

13 SUN   TWENTIETH SUNDAY AFTER TRINITY (OT 28)   Green
DWM 534 Gloria, Creed
Lec 143: Wis 7:7-11 ♦ Ps 90:12-17 ♦ Heb 4:12-13 ♦ Mk 10:17-30 or 10:17-27

MP Pss: 118   Lessons: Dn 6:1-23 ♦ Lk 12:22-34   Te Deum
EP 2   145   Ru 2:1-20a, 4:13-17 ♦ Phil 4

14 Mon   Feria   Green
Or:
St Callistus I, Pope and Martyr   *Red*
DWM 534
Lec 467: Gal 4:22-24, 26-27, 31-5:1 ♦ Lk 11:29-32
   Or, for St Callistus I, Pope and Martyr: DWM 857
Lec 656: 1 Pt 5:1-4 (#722.13) ♦ Lk 22:24-30 (#724.9)

MP Pss: 106:I   Lessons: Jb 27 ♦ Ti 1:1-2:8
EP   106:II   Jb 28 ♦ Heb 10:19-end

15 Tue   Saint Teresa of Jesus, Virgin and Doctor of the Church *Memorial*   White
DWM 858
Lec 468: Gal 5:1-6 ♦ Lk 11:37-41
   Or:
Lec 657: Rom 8:22-27 ♦ Jn 15:1-8 (#742.24)

MP Pss: 120-123   Lessons: Jb 29:1-30:1 ♦ Ti 2:9-3:end
EP   124-127   Jb 31:13-end ♦ Heb 11:1-16

16 Wed   USA: Feria   Green
Can: St Marguerite d'Youville, Religious *Memorial*   White
Or:
USA: *St Hedwig, Religious*   *White*
USA: *St Margaret Mary Alacoque, Virgin*   *White*
DWM (USA:) 534 (Can:) 944
Lec 469: Gal 5:18-25 ♦ Lk 11:42-46
   Or, for St Hedwig, Religious: DWM 858
Lec 658: Sir 26:1-4, 13-16 (#737.14) ♦ Mk 3:31-35 (#742.14)
   Or, for St Margaret Mary Alacoque, Virgin: DWM 859
Lec 659: Eph 3:14-19 (#740.7) ♦ Mt 11:25-30 (#742.4)

MP Pss: 119:XIX-XXII   Lessons: Jb 32 ♦ 2 Tm 1
EP   128-130   Jb 33 ♦ Heb 11:17-end

17 Thu   Saint Ignatius of Antioch, Bishop and Martyr *Memorial*   Red
DWM 859
Lec 470: Eph 1:1-10 ♦ Lk 11:47-54
    Or:
Lec 660: Phil 3:17-4:1 ♦ Jn 12:24-26 (#718.5)

MP	Pss: 131-133	Lessons:	Jb 38:1-21 ♦ 2 Tm 2
EP	134-135		Jb 38:22-end ♦ Heb 12:1-13

18 Fri   Saint Luke, Evangelist *Feast*   Red
DWM 861 Gloria
Lec 661: 2 Tm 4:10-17ab ♦ Ps 145:10-13, 17-18 ♦ Lk 10:1-9

MP	Pss: 103	Lessons:	Is 61:1-6 ♦ 2 Tm 3:10-end Te Deum
EP	67, 96 or 41, 43		Sir 38:1-14 or Is 55 ♦ Col 4:7-end or Lk 1:1-4

19 Sat   USA: Saints Jean de Brébeuf and Isaac Jogues, Priests, and Companions,   Red
Martyrs *Memorial*
    Can: Feria   Green
    Or:
    Can: *St Paul of the Cross, Priest*   *White*
    Can: *BVM: Mass of Saint Mary 5*   *White*
DWM (USA:) 862 (Can:) 534
USA: Lec 472: Eph 1:15-23 ♦ Lk 12:8-12
    Or:
USA: Lec 662: 2 Cor 4:7-15 (#716.3) ♦ Mt 28:16-20 (#724.4)
Can: Lec 472: Eph 1:15-23 ♦ Lk 12:8-12
    Or, for St Paul of the Cross, Priest: DWM 864
Lec 663: 1 Cor 1:18-25 (#722.2) ♦ Mt 16:24-27 (#742.6)
    Or, for Saint Mary: DWM 996
Lec 707-712 any readings from the Common of the BVM

MP	Pss: 137, 144	Lessons:	Jb 41 ♦ 2 Tm 4

EP 1 of The Twenty-first Sunday after Trinity

	Pss: 104	Lessons:	Jb 42 ♦ Heb 13

20 SUN   TWENTY-FIRST SUNDAY AFTER TRINITY (OT 29)   Green
DWM 536 Gloria, Creed
Lec 146: Is 53:10-11 ♦ Ps 33:3-5, 17-18, 19, 21 ♦ Heb 4:14-16 ♦ Mk 10:35-45 or 10:42-45

October 2024

MP Pss: 146-147   Lessons: 1 Mc 2:1-22 ♦ Lk 12:35-end   Te Deum

EP 2   111-113   Sir 3:17-29 ♦ 2 Cor 1:1-22

21 Mon   Feria   Green
DWM 536
Lec 473: Eph 2:1-10 ♦ Lk 12:13-21

MP Pss: 1-3   Lessons: Prv 1:1-19 ♦ Jas 1:1-11
EP   4, 7   Prv 1:20-end ♦ Jas 1:12-end

22 Tue   Feria   Green
            Or:
            St John Paul II, Pope   *White*
DWM 536
Lec 474: Eph 2:12-22 ♦ Lk 12:35-38
      Or, for St John Paul II, Pope: DWM 865
Lec 663A: Is 52:7-10 (#719.5) ♦ Jn 21:15-17 (#724.12)

MP Pss: 5-6   Lessons: Prv 2 ♦ Jas 2:1-13
EP   10-11   Prv 3:1-26 ♦ Jas 2:14-end

23 Wed   Feria   Green
            Or:
            St John of Capistrano, Priest   *White*
DWM 536
Lec 475: Eph 3:2-12 ♦ Lk 12:39-48
      Or, for St John of Capistrano, Priest: DWM 865
Lec 664: 2 Cor 5:14-20 (#722.7) ♦ Lk 9:57-62 (#742.19)

MP Pss: 119:I-III   Lessons: Prv 3:27-4:19 ♦ Jas 3
EP   12-14   Prv 4:20-5:14 ♦ Jas 4

24 Thu   Feria   Green
            Or:
            St Anthony Mary Claret, Bishop   *White*
DWM 536
Lec 476: Eph 3:14-21 ♦ Lk 12:49-53
      Or, for St Anthony Mary Claret, Bishop: DWM 866
Lec 665: Is 52:7-10 (#719.5) ♦ Mk 1:14-20 (#724.5)

MP Pss: 18:I   Lessons: Prv 6:1-19 ♦ Jas 5
EP   18:II   Prv 8 ♦ 1 Pt 1:1-12

October 2024

25 Fri   Feria   Green
DWM 536
Lec 477: Eph 4:1-6 ♦ Lk 12:54-59

MP Pss: 16-17   Lessons: Prv 9 ♦ 1 Pt 1:13-end
EP   22   Prv 10:1-22 ♦ 1 Pt 2:1-10

26 Sat   Feria   Green
Or:
BVM: Mass of Saint Mary 5   *White*
DWM 536
Lec 478: Eph 4:7-16 ♦ Lk 13:1-9
    Or, for Saint Mary: DWM 996
Lec 707-712 any readings from the Common of the BVM

MP Pss: 20-21   Lessons: Prv 11:1-25 ♦ 1 Pt 2:11-3:7
EP 1 of The Twenty-second Sunday after Trinity
    Pss: 110, 116-117   Lessons: Prv 12:10-end ♦ 1 Pt 3:8-end

27 SUN   TWENTY-SECOND SUNDAY AFTER TRINITY (OT 30)   Green
DWM 538 Gloria, Creed
Lec 149: Jer 31:7-9 ♦ Ps 126:1-7 ♦ Heb 5:1-6 ♦ Mk 10:46-52

MP Pss: 148-150   Lessons: 1 Mc 2:49-69 ♦ Lk   Te Deum
                         13:18-end
EP 2   114-115   Sir 4:11-28 ♦ 2 Cor 4

28 Mon   Saints Simon and Jude, Apostles *Feast*   Red
DWM 867 Gloria
Lec 666: Eph 2:19-22 ♦ Ps 19:1-4 ♦ Lk 6:12-19

MP Pss: 66   Lessons: Is 45:18-end ♦ Lk 6:12-19 Te Deum
EP   116-117 or 18:I   Jer 3:11-18 or Sir 15:11-20 ♦ Eph 2:11-end
                         or Jas 1:12-end

29 Tue   Feria   Green
DWM 538
Lec 480: Eph 5:21-33 ♦ Lk 13:18-21

MP Pss: 26, 28   Lessons: Prv 16:31-17:17 ♦ 1 Pt 5
EP   36, 39   Prv 18:10-end ♦ 1 Jn 1:1-2:6

30 Wed   Feria   Green

DWM 538

Lec 481: Eph 6:1-9 ♦ Lk 13:22-30

MP Pss: 38   Lessons: Prv 20:1-22 ♦ 1 Jn 2:7-17

EP   119:IV-VI   Prv 22:1-16 ♦ 1 Jn 2:18-end

31 Thu   Feria   Green

DWM 538

Lec 482: Eph 6:10-20 ♦ Lk 13:31-35

MP Pss: 37:I   Lessons: Prv 24:23-end ♦ 1 Jn 3:1-18

EP 1 of ALL SAINTS

      Pss: 34   Lessons: Is 65:17-end ♦ Heb 11:32-12:2

November 2024

1 Fri   ALL SAINTS' DAY *Solemnity* HDO   White
DWM 869 Gloria, Creed
Lec 667: Rv 7:2-4, 9-14 ♦ Ps 24:1-6, 9-10 ♦ 1 Jn 3:1-3 ♦ Mt 5:1-12a

MP   Pss: 111-112   Lessons: Wis 3:1-9 ♦ Rv 19:6-10   Te Deum
EP 2   148, 150   Sir 44:1-15 ♦ Heb 12:18-24

> ¶ Today being a *Solemnity*, the obligation to abstain from meat or to perform some other penitential act is dispensed (CIC 1251).

2 Sat   Commemoration of All the Faithful Departed   Black/Violet
DWM 871
Lec 668: Wis 3:1-9c (#1011.3) ♦ Rom 5:5-11 (#1014.1) or Rom 6:3-9 (#1014.3) ♦ Jn 6:37-40 (#1016.12); *or* any readings from Masses for the Dead, nos. 1011-1016

> ¶ On the norms to be observed in celebrating Masses for the Dead, see the Rubrical Directory, no. 45 (DWM 130).
>
> ¶ "On All Souls' Day, the Sequence *Dies irae* may be sung or said" after the Tract (DWM 872).
>
> ¶ "On this day, any Priest may celebrate three Masses, observing, nevertheless, what was established by Benedict XV in the Apostolic Constitution, *Incruentum altaris sacrificium*, 10 August 1915: *Acta Apostolicae Sedis* 7 (1915) pp. 401-404" (DWM 871).
>
> ¶ The preferred readings for celebrating All Souls' Day in the Personal Ordinariate of the Chair of Saint Peter are given above. These are the primary readings given in lectionaries and people's missals published under the direction of the USCCB. By using these readings, we read together with the wider Church nearby. These readings appear in Volume II of the RSV-2CE lectionary, as indicated. Other readings from Masses for the Dead, nos. 1011-1016, may also be used, including those on pages 963-965 of Volume I of the RSV-2CE lectionary. The readings in Volume I were selected from among the permitted readings at the recommendation of the Conference of Catholic Bishops of the Antilles, who published the RSV-2CE lectionary. Sacristans and Readers should consult with the Celebrant or Homilist to ascertain the desired reading before setting the book and before reading.

MP   Pss: 27, 90:1-12   Lessons: Is 43:1-7 ♦ Jn 5:24-29
EP   130, 139:1-11   Jb 19:21-27a ♦ Rv 1:9-18

3 SUN   TWENTY-THIRD SUNDAY AFTER TRINITY (OT 31)   Green
DWM 540 Gloria, Creed
Lec 152: Dt 6:2-6 ♦ Ps 18:1-3, 47, 51 ♦ Heb 7:23-28 ♦ Mk 12:28b-34

MP   Pss: 63, 98   Lessons: 1 Mc 3:42-end ♦ Lk   Te Deum
                                   14:15-end
EP   103   Sir 4:29-6:1 ♦ 2 Cor 5

November 2024

4 Mon   Saint Charles Borromeo, Bishop *Memorial*   White
DWM 876
Lec 485: Phil 2:1-4 ♦ Lk 14:12-14
    Or:
Lec 670: Rom 12:3-13 (#722.1) ♦ Jn 10:11-16 (#724.10)

MP Pss: 41, 52   Lessons: Sir 1:1-10 ♦ Acts 1
EP   44   Sir 1:11-end ♦ Acts 2:1-21

5 Tue   Feria   Green
DWM 540
Lec 486: Phil 2:5-11 ♦ Lk 14:15-24

MP Pss: 45   Lessons: Sir 2 ♦ Acts 2:22-end
EP   47-48   Sir 3:17-29 ♦ Acts 3:1-4:4

6 Wed   Feria   Green
DWM 540
Lec 487: Phil 2:12-18 ♦ Lk 14:25-33

MP Pss: 119:VII-IX   Lessons: Sir 4:11-28 ♦ Acts 4:5-31
EP   49, 53   Sir 4:29-6:1 ♦ Acts 4:32-5:11

7 Thu   Feria   Green
DWM 540
Lec 488: Phil 3:3-8a ♦ Lk 15:1-10

MP Pss: 50   Lessons: Sir 6:14-31 ♦ Acts 5:12-end
EP   59-60   Sir 7:27-end ♦ Acts 6:1-7:16

8 Fri   Feria   Green
DWM 540
Lec 489: Phil 3:17-4:1 ♦ Lk 16:1-8

MP Pss: 40, 54   Lessons: Sir 10:6-8,12-24 ♦ Acts 7:17-34
EP   51   Sir 11:7-28 ♦ Acts 7:35-8:4

9 Sat   Dedication of the Lateran Basilica *Feast*   White
DWM 879 Gloria
Lec 671: Ez 47:1-2, 8-9, 12 (#701.5) ♦ Ps 46:1-2, 4-5, 7-8 ♦ 1 Cor 3:9c-11, 16-17
(#704.1) ♦ Jn 2:13-22 (#706.3)

MP	Pss: 84, 87	Lessons: 2 Chr 5:6-10, 13-6:2 ♦ 1 Pt 2:4-9	Te Deum
EP	95:1-7, 122	Is 6 ♦ Mt 5:21-37	

10 SUN   TWENTY-FOURTH SUNDAY AFTER TRINITY (OT 32)   Green
DWM 542 Gloria, Creed
Lec 155: 1 Kgs 17:10-16 ♦ Ps 146:1, 4-10 ♦ Heb 9:24-28 ♦ Mk 12:38-44 or 12:41-44

MP	Pss: 24, 29	Lessons: 1 Mc 14:4-15 ♦ Lk 15:1-10 Te Deum
EP	8, 84	Sir 11:7-28 ♦ 2 Cor 9

11 Mon   Saint Martin of Tours, Bishop *Memorial*   White
Or:
Can: *Remembrance Day*   *Black/Violet*
DWM 881
Lec 491: Ti 1:1-9 ♦ Lk 17:1-6
   Or:
Lec 673: Is 61:1-3abcd (#719.6) ♦ Mt 25:31-40 (#742.13 shorter)
   Or, for Remembrance Day: DWM 1022
Lec 668 or 1011-1016: any appropriate readings from The Commemoration of
all the Faithful Departed or from the Masses for the Dead

¶ On the norms to be observed in celebrating Masses for the Dead, see the Rubrical
Directory, no. 45 (DWM 130).

MP	Pss: 56-58	Lessons: Sir 16:17-end ♦ Acts 9:1-31
EP	64-65	Sir 17:1-24 ♦ Acts 9:32-end

12 Tue   Saint Josaphat, Bishop and Martyr *Memorial*   Red
DWM 881
Lec 492: Ti 2:1-8, 11-14 ♦ Lk 17:7-10
   Or:
Lec 674: Eph 4:1-7, 11-13 (#722.8) ♦ Jn 17:20-26 (#742.26)

MP	Pss: 61-62	Lessons: Sir 18:1-14 ♦ Acts 10:1-23
EP	68	Sir 19:13-end ♦ Acts 10:24-end

13 Wed   USA: Saint Frances Xavier Cabrini, Virgin *Memorial*   White
Can: Feria   Green
DWM (USA:) 882 (Can:) 542
Lec 493: Ti 3:1-7 ♦ Lk 17:11-19

MP	Pss: 72	Lessons: Sir 21:1-17 ♦ Acts 11:1-18
EP	119:X-XII	Sir 22:6-22 ♦ Acts 11:19-end

14 Thu   Feria   Green
DWM 542
Lec 494: Phlm 7-20 ♦ Lk 17:20-25

MP Pss: 70-71   Lessons: Sir 22:27-23:15 ♦ Acts 12:1-24
EP   74   Sir 24:1-22 ♦ Acts 12:25-13:12

15 Fri   Feria   Green
Or:
St Albert the Great, Bishop and Doctor of the Church   *White*
DWM 542
Lec 495: 2 Jn 4-9 ♦ Lk 17:26-37
Or, for St Albert the Great, Bishop and Doctor of the Church: DWM 883
Lec 675: Sir 15:1-6 (#725.3) ♦ Mt 13:47-52 (#730.3)

MP Pss: 69   Lessons: Sir 24:23-end ♦ Acts 13:13-43
EP   73   Sir 27:30-28:9 ♦ Acts 13:44-14:7

16 Sat   Feria   Green
Or:
St Margaret of Scotland   *White*
St Gertrude, Virgin   *White*
BVM: Mass of Saint Mary 5   *White*
DWM 542
Lec 496: 3 Jn 5-8 ♦ Lk 18:1-8
Or, for St Margaret of Scotland: DWM 883
Lec 676: Is 58:6-11 (#737.15) ♦ Jn 15:9-17 (#742.25)
Or, for St Gertrude, Virgin: DWM 883
Lec 677: Eph 3:14-19 (#740.7) ♦ Jn 15:1-8 (#742.24)
Or, for Saint Mary: DWM 996
Lec 707-712 any readings from the Common of the BVM

MP Pss: 75-76   Lessons: Sir 31:1-11 ♦ Acts 14:8-end
EP 1 of The Twenty-fifth Sunday after Trinity
      Pss: 23, 27   Lessons: Sir 34:9-end ♦ Acts 15:1-21

17 SUN   TWENTY-FIFTH SUNDAY AFTER TRINITY (OT 33)   Green
DWM 544 Gloria, Creed
Lec 158: Dn 12:1-3 ♦ Ps 16:1, 6, 9-12 ♦ Heb 10:11-14, 18 ♦ Mk 13:24-32

MP Pss: 93, 96   Lessons: Sir 15:11-end ♦ Lk   Te Deum
17:1-10

EP 2   34   Sir 27:30-28:9 ♦ 1 Tm 6:1-16 (17-end)

18 Mon   Feria   Green
Or:
Dedication of the Basilicas of Sts Peter and Paul, Apostles   *White*
USA: *St Rose Philippine Duchesne, Virgin*   *White*
DWM 544
Lec 497: Rv 1:1-4; 2:1-5a ♦ Lk 18:35-43
    Or, for Dedication of the Basilicas of Sts Peter and Paul, Apostles: DWM 885
Lec 679: **Acts 28:11-16, 30-31** ♦ Ps 98:1-7 ♦ **Mt 14:22-33**
    Or, for St Rose Philippine Duchesne, Virgin: DWM 886

MP Pss: 80   Lessons: Eccl 1 ♦ Acts 15:22-35
EP   77, 79   Eccl 2:1-23 ♦ Acts 15:36-16:5

19 Tue   Feria   Green
DWM 544
Lec 498: Rv 3:1-6, 14-22 ♦ Lk 19:1-10

MP Pss: 78:I   Lessons: Eccl 3:1-15 ♦ Acts 16:6-end
EP   78:II   Eccl 3:16-4:6 ♦ Acts 17:1-15

20 Wed   Feria   Green
Or:
St Edmund, Martyr   *Red*
DWM 544
Lec 499: Rv 4:1-11 ♦ Lk 19:11-28
    Or, for St Edmund, Martyr: DWM 886

MP Pss: 119:XIII-XV   Lessons: Eccl 4:7-end ♦ Acts 17:16-end
EP   81-82   Eccl 5 ♦ Acts 18:1-23

21 Thu   The Presentation of the Blessed Virgin Mary *Memorial*   White
DWM 887
Lec 500: Rv 5:1-10 ♦ Lk 19:41-44
    Or:
Lec 680: Zec 2:10-13 (#707.11) ♦ Mt 12:46-50 (#712.3)

MP Pss: 83   Lessons: Eccl 6 ♦ Acts 18:24-19:7
EP   85-86   Eccl 7:1-14 ♦ Acts 19:8-20

22 Fri   Saint Cecilia, Virgin and Martyr *Memorial*   Red

DWM 888

Lec 501: Rv 10:8-11 ♦ Lk 19:45-48

    Or:

Lec 681: Hos 2:14bc, 15cd, 19-20 (#731.2) ♦ Mt 25:1-13 (#736.2)

MP Pss: 88   Lessons: Eccl 7:15-end ♦ Acts 19:21-end

EP   91-92   Eccl 8 ♦ Acts 20:1-16

23 Sat   Feria   Green

           Or:

           Bl Miguel Agustín Pro, Priest and Martyr   *Red*

           St Clement I, Pope and Martyr   *Red*

           St Columban, Abbot   *White*

           BVM: Mass of Saint Mary 5   *White*

DWM 544

Lec 502: Rv 11:4-12 ♦ Lk 20:27-40

    Or, for Bl Miguel Agustín Pro, Priest and Martyr: DWM 889

    Or, for St Clement I, Pope and Martyr: DWM 888

Lec 682: 1 Pt 5:1-4 (#722.13) ♦ Mt 16:13-19 (#724.2)

    Or, for St Columban, Abbot: DWM 889

Lec 683: Is 52:7-10 (#719.5) ♦ Lk 9:57-62 (#742.19)

    Or, for Saint Mary: DWM 996

Lec 707-712 any readings from the Common of the BVM

MP Pss: 87, 90   Lessons: Eccl 9 ♦ Acts 20:17-end

EP 1 of Christ the King

      Pss: 136   Lessons: Eccl 10:5-18 ♦ Acts 21:1-16

24 SUN   OUR LORD JESUS CHRIST, KING OF THE UNIVERSE COMMONLY   White
          CALLED CHRIST THE KING *Solemnity*

DWM 546 Gloria, Creed

Lec 161: Dn 7:13-14 ♦ Ps 93:1-3, 6 ♦ Rv 1:5-8 ♦ Jn 18:33b-37

MP Pss: 118   Lessons: Eccl 11 & 12 ♦ Heb   Te Deum
                          11:1-16

EP 2   145   Mal 3:1-6 & 4 ♦ Heb 11:17-12:2

25 Mon   Weekday Before Advent   Green

           Or:

           St Catherine of Alexandria, Virgin and Martyr   *Red*

DWM 548

Lec 503: Rv 14:1-3, 4b-5 ♦ Lk 21:1-4

November 2024

Or, for St Catherine of Alexandria, Virgin and Martyr: DWM 890

MP	Pss: 106:I	Lessons:	Wis 1 ♦ Mt 5:1-16
EP	106:II		Wis 2 ♦ Rv 1

26 Tue   Weekday Before Advent   Green
DWM 548
Lec 504: Rv 14:14-19 ♦ Lk 21:5-11

† The Rev. Michael Birch, November 26, 2016.

MP	Pss: 120-123	Lessons:	Wis 3:1-9 ♦ Mt 5:17-end
EP	124-127		Wis 4:7-end ♦ Rv 2:1-17

27 Wed   Weekday Before Advent   Green
DWM 548
Lec 505: Rv 15:1-4 ♦ Lk 21:12-19

MP	Pss: 119:XIX-XXII	Lessons:	Wis 5:1-16 ♦ Mt 6:1-18
EP	128-130		Wis 6:1-21 ♦ Rv 2:18-3:6

28 Thu   Weekday Before Advent   Green
     Or:
     Thanksgiving Day [US]   *White*
DWM 548
Lec 506: Rv 18:1-2, 21-23; 19:1-3, 9a ♦ Lk 21:20-28
     Or, for Thanksgiving Day [US]: DWM 1020
Lec 943-947: any readings from the Mass In Thanksgiving to God

MP	Pss: 131-133	Lessons:	Wis 7:15-8:4 ♦ Mt 6:19-end
EP	134-135		Wis 8:5-18 ♦ Rv 3:7-end

29 Fri   Weekday Before Advent   Green
DWM 548
Lec 507: Rv 20:1-4, 11-21:2 ♦ Lk 21:29-33

MP	Pss: 140, 142	Lessons:	Wis 8:21-9:end ♦ Mt 7:1-14
EP	141, 143		Wis 10:15-11:10 ♦ Rv 4

30 Sat   Saint Andrew, Apostle *Feast*   Red
DWM 891 Gloria
Lec 684: Rom 10:9-18 ♦ Ps 19:1-4 ♦ Mt 4:18-22

MP Pss: 34   Lessons: Is 49:1-9a ♦ Jn 1:35-42   Te Deum

EP 1 of The First Sunday of Advent

     Pss: 104   Lessons: Wis 12:12-21 ♦ Rv 5

December 2024

Lectionary Cycle:
Year C - Weekdays Year I - Daily Office Year I

1 SUN   FIRST SUNDAY OF ADVENT   Violet

DWM 152 Creed

Lec 3: Jer 33:14-16 ♦ Ps 25:3-4, 7-9, 13 ♦ 1 Thes 3:12-4:2 ♦ Lk 21:25-28, 34-36

> ¶ The Litany may be sung in procession before the principal Sunday Mass (DWM 1061).
> ¶ The Advent Prose may be sung on any of the Sundays of Advent (DWM 151).

MP Pss: 146-147   Lessons: Is 1:1-20 ♦ Mt 24:1-28   Te Deum
EP 2   111-113   Is 2:10-end ♦ 1 Thes 5

> ¶ *Alma Redemptoris Mater* may be said after EP or Compline from Advent through Candlemas.

2 Mon   Advent Feria   Violet

DWM 152

Lec 175: Is 2:1-5 ♦ Mt 8:5-11

MP Pss: 1-3   Lessons: Is 3:1-15 ♦ Mk 1:1-20
EP   4, 7   Is 4:2-end ♦ Rv 6

3 Tue   Saint Francis Xavier, Priest *Memorial*   White

DWM 893

Lec 176: Is 11:1-10 ♦ Lk 10:21-24
    Or:
Lec 685: 1 Cor 9:16-19, 22-23 (#722.4) ♦ Mk 16:15-20 (#724.6)

MP Pss: 5-6   Lessons: Is 5:1-17 ♦ Mk 1:21-end
EP   10-11   Is 5:18-end ♦ Rv 7

4 Wed   Ember Wednesday in Advent   Violet
    [*St John Damascene, Priest and Doctor of the Church*]

DWM 154

Lec 177: Is 25:6-10a ♦ Mt 15:29-37

St John Damascene, Priest and Doctor of the Church may optionally be commemorated only in the Daily Office by adding the DWM 894 Collect after the Collect of the Day.

MP Pss: 119:I-III   Lessons: Is 6 ♦ Mk 2:1-22
EP   12-14   Is 8:16-9:7 ♦ Rv 8

5 Thu	Advent Feria	Violet

DWM 152

Lec 178: Is 26:1-6 ♦ Mt 7:21, 24-27

MP	Pss: 18:I	Lessons:	Is 9:8-10:4 ♦ Mk 2:23-3:12
EP	18:II		Is 10:5-23 ♦ Rv 9

6 Fri	Ember Friday in Advent	Violet

[*St Nicholas, Bishop*]

DWM 155

Lec 179: Is 29:17-24 ♦ Mt 9:27-31

St Nicholas, Bishop may optionally be commemorated only in the Daily Office
by adding the DWM 894 Collect after the Collect of the Day.

> ❖ On the recommendation of the Governing Council, the Bishop has decreed that Ember
> Friday in Advent is to be kept as an obligatory day of abstinence.

MP	Pss: 16-17	Lessons:	Is 10:24-11:9 ♦ Mk 3:13-end
EP	22		Is 11:10-12:end ♦ Rv 10

7 Sat	Ember Saturday in Advent, or	Violet
	St Ambrose, Bishop and Doctor of the Church *Memorial*	White

DWM 156 or 895

Lec 180: Is 30:19-21, 23-26 ♦ Mt 9:35-10:1, 5a, 6-8
   Or:
Lec 688: Eph 3:8-12 (#728.4) ♦ Jn 10:11-16 (#724.10)

MP	Pss: 20-21	Lessons:	Is 13:1-14:2 ♦ Mk 4:1-20

EP 1 of The Second Sunday of Advent
   Pss: 110, 116-117   Lessons: Is 14:3-27 ♦ Rv 11

8 SUN	SECOND SUNDAY OF ADVENT	Violet

DWM 158 Creed

Lec 6: Bar 5:1-9 ♦ Ps 126:1-7 ♦ Phil 1:4-6, 8-11 ♦ Lk 3:1-6

MP	Pss: 148-150	Lessons:	Is 5:1-16 ♦ Mt 24:29-end	Te Deum
EP 2	114-115		Is 5:18-end ♦ 2 Tm 3:14-4:8	

9 Mon	IMMACULATE CONCEPTION OF THE BLESSED VIRGIN MARY	White
	Solemnity (Patronal Feastday of the USA)	

DWM 896 Gloria, Creed

Lec 689: Gn 3:9-15, 20 ♦ Ps 98:1-5 ♦ Eph 1:3-6, 11-12 ♦ Lk 1:26-38

> ¶ This year the Solemnity of the Immaculate Conception is transferred to December 9th, and the obligation to attend Mass is abrogated. Because the Immaculate Conception is the Patronal Feastday of the USA, the precept to attend Mass applies even in years where 8 December falls on a Monday or Saturday (general decree of the USCCB, December 13, 1991, and CIC 1246), but it does not apply in years when the Solemnity is transferred to Monday, December 9th.

MP	Pss: 63, 100	Lessons:	Is 61:10-62:5 ♦ 1 Cor 1:26-30	Te Deum
EP	45, 93		Zep 3:14-17 ♦ Rv 11:19, 12:1-6, 10	

10 Tue   Advent Feria   *Violet*
Or:
Our Lady of Loreto   *White*
DWM 158
Lec 182: Is 40:1-11 ♦ Mt 18:12-14
Or, for Our Lady of Loreto: DWM 913
Lec 707-712 any reading from the Common of the Blessed Virgin Mary

MP	Pss: 26, 28	Lessons:	Is 19:1-17 ♦ Mk 5:1-20
EP	36, 39		Is 19:18-end ♦ Rv 13

11 Wed   Advent Feria   *Violet*
Or:
St Damasus I, Pope   *White*
DWM 158
Lec 183: Is 40:25-31 ♦ Mt 11:28-30
Or, for St Damasus I, Pope: DWM 898
Lec 690: Acts 20:17-18a, 28-32, 36 (#720.2) ♦ Jn 15:9-17 (#724.11)

MP	Pss: 38	Lessons:	Is 21:1-12 ♦ Mk 5:21-end
EP	119:IV-VI		Is 22:1-14 ♦ Rv 14

12 Thu   Our Lady of Guadalupe *Feast*   White
DWM 899 Gloria
Lec 690A: Zec 2:10-13 (#707.11), or Rv 11:19a; 12:1-6a, 10ab (#708.2) ♦ Lk 1:26-38 (#712.4), or Lk 1:39-47 (#712.5)

MP	Pss: 24, 46	Lessons:	Gn 12:1-7 ♦ Lk 11:27-28	Te Deum
EP	87, 95		Zec 2:1-13 ♦ Eph 1:3-12	

13 Fri   Saint Lucy, Virgin and Martyr *Memorial*   Red
DWM 900
Lec 185: Is 48:17-19 ♦ Mt 11:16-19

Or:
Lec 692: 2 Cor 10:17-11:2 (#734.2) ♦ Mt 25:1-13 (#736.2)

MP	Pss: 31	Lessons:	Is 28:14-end ♦ Mk 6:14-29
EP	35		Is 29:1-14 ♦ Rv 16

14 Sat   Saint John of the Cross, Priest and Doctor of the Church *Memorial*   White
DWM 901
Lec 186: Sir 48:1-4, 9-11b ♦ Mt 17:10-13
    Or:
Lec 693: 1 Cor 2:1-10a (#728.2) ♦ Lk 14:25-33 (#742.23)

MP Pss: 30, 32   Lessons: Is 29:15-end ♦ Mk 6:30-end
EP 1 of The Third Sunday of Advent
        Pss: 42-43   Lessons: Is 30:1-18 ♦ Rv 17

15 SUN   THIRD SUNDAY OF ADVENT   Rose/Violet
DWM 160 Creed
Lec 9: Zep 3:14-18a ♦ Isaiah 12:2-6 (DWDO 74) ♦ Phil 4:4-7 ♦ Lk 3:10-18

MP Pss: 63, 98   Lessons: Is 25:1-9 ♦ Mt 25:1-30   Te Deum
EP 2   103   Is 26:1-13 ♦ 1 Tm 1:12-2:8

16 Mon   Advent Feria   Violet
DWM 160
Lec 187: Nm 24:2-7, 15-17a ♦ Mt 21:23-27

MP Pss: 41, 52   Lessons: Is 30:19-end ♦ Mk 7:1-23
EP   44   Is 31 ♦ Rv 18

17 Tue   17 December (O Sapientia)   Violet
DWM 166
Lec 193: Gn 49:2, 8-10 ♦ Mt 1:1-17

> ¶ "On the appointed days, these [Advent] Anthems following are sung or said before and after [as antiphons on] the *Magnificat* at Evening Prayer," beginning with *O Sapientia* on 17 December (DWM 162).

MP Pss: 45   Lessons: Is 38:1-20 ♦ Mk 7:24-8:10
EP   47-48   Is 40:1-11 ♦ Rv 19

| 18 Wed | 18 December (O Adonai) | | Violet |

DWM 168

Lec 194: Jer 23:5-8 ♦ Mt 1:18-24

| MP | Pss: 119:VII-IX | Lessons: | Is 40:12-end ♦ Mk 8:11-9:1 |
| EP | 49, 53 | | Is 41 ♦ Rv 20 |

| 19 Thu | 19 December (O Radix Jesse) | | Violet |

DWM 170

Lec 195: Jgs 13:2-7, 24-25a ♦ Lk 1:5-25

| MP | Pss: 50 | Lessons: | Is 42:1-17 ♦ Mk 9:2-32 |
| EP | 33 | | Is 42:18-43:13 ♦ Rv 21:1-14 |

| 20 Fri | 20 December (O Clavis David) | | Violet |

DWM 172

Lec 196: Is 7:10-14 ♦ Lk 1:26-38

| MP | Pss: 40, 54 | Lessons: | Is 43:14-44:5 ♦ Mk 9:33-end |
| EP | 51 | | Is 44:6-23 ♦ Rv 21:15-22:5 |

| 21 Sat | 21 December (O Oriens) | | Violet |

[*St Peter Canisius, Priest and Doctor of the Church*]

DWM 174

Lec 197: Sg 2:8-14 or Zep 3:14-18a ♦ Lk 1:39-45

Or, for St Peter Canisius, Priest and Doctor of the Church: DWM 901 – if commemorated, Collect only

| MP | Pss: 55 | Lessons: | Is 44:24-45:13 ♦ Mk 10:1-31 |

EP 1 of The Fourth Sunday of Advent

| | Pss: 138-139 | Lessons: | Is 45:14-end ♦ Rv 22:6-end |

| 22 SUN | FOURTH SUNDAY OF ADVENT [O Rex Gentium] | | Violet |

DWM 164 Creed

Lec 12: Mi 5:2-5a ♦ Ps 80:1-3, 14-15, 17-19 ♦ Heb 10:5-10 ♦ Lk 1:39-45

| MP | Pss: 24, 29 | Lessons: | Is 32:1-8 ♦ Mt 25:31-end | Te Deum |
| EP 2 | 8, 84 | | Is 40:1-11 ♦ 2 Pt 3:1-14 | |

| 23 Mon | 23 December (O Emmanuel) | | Violet |

[*St John of Kanty, Priest*]

DWM 178

Lec 199: Mal 3:1-4, 4:5-6 ♦ Lk 1:57-66

Or, for St John of Kanty, Priest: DWM 902 – if commemorated, Collect only

MP Pss: 61-62   Lessons: Is 46 ♦ Mk 10:32-end
EP   112, 115   Is 47 ♦ Jude 1-16

24 Tue   24 December Morning (O Virgo Virginum)   Violet
              In the evening:
              THE VIGIL OF THE NATIVITY (Christmas Eve)   *White*
              DWM 180
              Lec 200: 2 Sm 7:1-5, 8b-12, 14a, 16 ♦ Lk 1:67-79
              Or, for Christmas Eve: See Vigil Mass below.

MP Pss: 45-46   Lessons: Is 48 ♦ Mk 11:1-26
EP 1 of Christmas
      Pss: 89:I   Lessons: Zec 2:10-end ♦ Ti 2:11-3:7

> ¶ The Proclamation of the Nativity of Our Lord Jesus Christ "may be chanted or recited, most appropriately on 24th December, at Evening Prayer" (DWM 1069). Otherwise, the Proclamation may be made before the Christmas Mass during the Night.

25 Wed   NATIVITY OF THE LORD *Solemnity* HDO   White
              Vigil Mass (Masses on Christmas Eve which begin before 10:00 PM)
              DWM 184 Gloria, Creed
              Lec 13: Is 62:1-5 ♦ Ps 89:1, 3-4, 16-17, 27, 29 ♦ Acts 13:16-17, 22-25 ♦ Mt 1:1-25 or 1:18-25
              Mass In the Night (Masses on Christmas Eve which begin at 10:00 PM or later)
              DWM 186 Gloria, Creed
              Lec 14: Is 9:2-7 ♦ Ps 96:1-3, 11-13 ♦ Ti 2:11-14 ♦ Lk 2:1-14

> ¶ The Proclamation of the Nativity of Our Lord Jesus Christ may "be chanted or recited before the beginning of the Christmas Mass during the Night. It may not replace any part of the Mass" (DWM 1069).

Mass at Dawn (Masses on Christmas Day which begin before 9:00 AM)
DWM 188 Gloria, Creed
Lec 15: Is 62:11-12 ♦ Ps 97:1, 6, 11-12 ♦ Ti 3:4-7 ♦ Lk 2:15-20
Mass on the Day (Masses on Christmas Day which begin at 9:00 AM or later)
DWM 190 Gloria, Creed
Lec 16: Is 52:7-10 ♦ Ps 98:1-7 ♦ Heb 1:1-6 ♦ Jn 1:1-18 or 1:1-5, 9-14

> ¶ The Last Gospel "is especially appropriate in Christmastide, until the Baptism of the Lord or until Candlemas."
> ¶ Following the Mass During the Day, when the Prologue of John is the Gospel of the Mass, Lec 20: Matthew 2:1-12 may be read as the Last Gospel in place of the Prologue (DWM 1058).

December 2024

MP   Pss: 2, 85   Lessons: Is 9:2-7 ♦ Lk 2:1-20   Te Deum
EP 2   110, 132   Is 7:10-14 ♦ 1 Jn 4:7-end

26 Thu   Saint Stephen, the First Martyr *Feast*   Red
DWM 902 Gloria
Lec 696: Acts 6:8-10; 7:54-59 ♦ Ps 31:3-4, 6,8, 17-18 ♦ Mt 10:17-22

MP   Pss: 28, 30   Lessons: Gn 4:1-10 ♦ Acts 6   Te Deum
EP   118   Ex 18:13-26 or Is 49:14-25 ♦ Acts 7:59-8:8

27 Fri   Saint John, Apostle and Evangelist *Feast*   White
DWM 904 Gloria
Lec 697: 1 Jn 1:1-4 ♦ Ps 97:1-2, 5-6, 11-12 ♦ Jn 20:2-8

MP   Pss: 97-98   Lessons: Ex 33:9-19 ♦ Jn 13:21-35   Te Deum
EP   145   Is 6:1-8 ♦ 1 Jn 5:1-12

28 Sat   Holy Innocents, Martyrs *Feast*   Red
DWM 905 Gloria
Lec 698: 1 Jn 1:5-2:2 ♦ Ps 124:1-4, 6-7 ♦ Mt 2:13-18

MP   Pss: 2, 26   Lessons: Jer 31:1-17 ♦ Mt 18:1-10   Te Deum
EP 1 of The Holy Family
     Pss: 23, 27   Lessons: Nm 6:22-26 ♦ Lk 21:25-36

29 SUN   HOLY FAMILY OF JESUS, MARY AND JOSEPH *Feast*   White
DWM 192 Gloria, Creed
Lec 17: 1 Sm 1:20-22, 24-28 or Sir 3:2-6, 12-14 ♦ Ps 84:1-2, 4-5, 8-11 or Ps 128:1-6 ♦
1 Jn 3:1-2, 21-24 or Col 3:12-21 ♦ Lk 2:41-52

> ¶ The first reading, psalm, and second reading from Year A may be used in Years B and C. The Gospel for each year is proper. The Year C readings are listed first in the citation above. In the RSV-2CE lectionary, the Year A first and second readings are given first, beginning on page 595, followed by the proper Gospel for Year C. The Year C readings, including a duplicate copy of the proper Gospel, begin on page 598 of the Lectionary. Sacristans and Readers should consult with the Celebrant or Homilist to ascertain the desired reading before setting the book and before reading.

MP   Pss: 93, 96   Lessons: Is 41:8-20 ♦ Col 1:1-20   Te Deum
EP 2   34   Is 12 ♦ Phil 2:1-11

30 Mon   Sixth Day in the Octave of Christmas   White
DWM 190
Lec 203: 1 Jn 2:12-17 ♦ Lk 2:36-40

MP Pss: 20-21   Lessons: Is 60:13-end ♦ Jn 3:16-21   Te Deum
EP   23,27   Is 61 ♦ Mt 16:13-20

31 Tue   Seventh Day in the Octave of Christmas   White
        [*St Sylvester I, Pope*]
        DWM 190
        Lec 204: 1 Jn 2:18-21 ♦ Jn 1:1-18
                Or, for St Sylvester I, Pope: DWM 908 – if commemorated, Collect only

        MP Pss: 46, 48   Lessons: Is 62 ♦ Jn 6:41-58   Te Deum
        EP 1 of Mary, Mother of God
                Pss: 90   Lessons: Is 65:15b-25 ♦ Rv 21:1-6

APPENDICES

1. *Abbreviations of the Books of the Bible*

OLD TESTAMENT

Amos	Am		Kings	1 Kgs
Baruch	Bar		2 Kings	2 Kgs
1 Chronicles	1 Chr		Lamentations	Lam
2 Chronicles	2 Chr		Leviticus	Lv
Daniel	Dn		1 Maccabees	1 Mc
Deuteronomy	Dt		2 Maccabees	2 Mc
Ecclesiastes	Eccl		Malachi	Mal
Esther	Est		Micah	Mi
Exodus	Ex		Nahum	Na
Ezra	Ezr		Nehemiah	Neh
Ezekiel	Ez		Numbers	Nm
Genesis	Gn		Obadiah	Ob
Habakkuk	Hb		Proverbs	Prv
Haggai	Hg		Psalm(s)	Ps(s)
Hosea	Hos		Ruth	Ru
Isaiah	Is		1 Samuel	1 Sm
Jeremiah	Jer		2 Samuel	2 Sm
Job	Jb		Sirach	Sir
Joel	Jl		Song of Songs	Sg
Jonah	Jon		Tobit	Tb
Joshua	Jos		Wisdom	Wis
Judges	Jgs		Zechariah	Zec
Judith	Jdt		Zephaniah	Zep

NEW TESTAMENT

Acts of the Apostles	Acts		Mark	Mk
Colossians	Col		Matthew	Mt
1 Corinthians	1 Cor		1 Peter	1 Pt
2 Corinthians	2 Cor		2 Peter	2 Pt
Ephesians	Eph		Philemon	Phlm
Galatians	Gal		Philippians	Phil
Hebrews	Heb		Revelation	Rv
James	Jas		Romans	Rom
John (Gospel)	Jn		1 Thessalonians	1 Thes
1 John	1 Jn		2 Thessalonians	2 Thes
2 John	2 Jn		1 Timothy	1 Tm
3 John	3 Jn		2 Timothy	2 Tm
Jude	Jude		Titus	Ti
Luke	Lk			

2. *Table of Liturgical Days according to their order of precedence*
(DWM 132-134)

I

1. The Paschal Triduum of the Passion and Resurrection of the Lord.

2. The Nativity of the Lord, the Epiphany, the Ascension, and Pentecost.
   Sundays of Advent, Sundays in Lent, and Sundays of Easter.
   Ash Wednesday.
   Weekdays of Holy Week from Monday up to and including Thursday.
   Days within the Octave of Easter.

3. Solemnities inscribed in the General Calendar, whether of the Lord, of the Blessed Virgin Mary, or of Saints.
   The Commemoration of All the Faithful Departed (All Souls).

4. Proper Solemnities, namely:
   a) The Solemnity of the Title of the Ordinariate.
   b) The Solemnity of the principal Patron of the place, city, or state.
   c) The Solemnity of the dedication and of the anniversary of the dedication of one's own church.
   d) The Solemnity of the Title of one's own church.
   e) The Solemnity either of the Title or of the Founder or of the principal Patron of an Order or Congregation.

II

5. Feasts of the Lord inscribed in the General Calendar.

6. Sundays of Christmas Time, the Sundays after Epiphany,
   Septuagesima, Sexagesima, Quinquagesima, the Sundays after Trinity.

7. Feasts of the Blessed Virgin Mary and of the Saints in the General Calendar.

8. Proper Feasts, namely:
   a) The Feast of the principal Patron of the Ordinariate.
   b) The Feast of the anniversary of the dedication of the principal church of the Ordinariate.
   c) The Feast of the principal Patron of a region or province, or a country, or of a wider territory.
   d) The Feast of the Title, Founder, or principal Patron of an Order or Congregation and of a religious province, without prejudice to the prescriptions given under no. 4.
   e) Other Feasts proper to an individual church.
   f) Other Feasts inscribed in the Calendar of each Ordinariate.

9. Weekdays of Advent from 17th December up to and including 24th December.
   Days within the Octave of Christmas.
   Days within the Octave of Pentecost (including the Ember Days therein).
   Weekdays of Lent.

10.   Obligatory Memorials in the General Calendar.
        Ember Days.
        Rogation Days.

11.   Proper Obligatory Memorials, namely:
        a) The Memorial of a secondary Patron of the place, Ordinariate, region, or religious province.
        b) Other Obligatory Memorials inscribed in the Calendar of each Ordinariate, or Order or congregation.

12.   Optional Memorials, which, however, may be celebrated, in the special manner described in the *General Instruction of the Roman Missal*, even on the days listed in no. 9.
        In the same manner Obligatory Memorials may be celebrated as Optional Memorials if they happen to fall on Lenten weekdays.

13.   Weekdays of Advent up to and including 16th December.
        Weekdays of Christmas Time from 2nd January until the Saturday after the Epiphany.
        Weekdays of the Easter Time from Monday after the Octave of Easter up to and including the Saturday before Pentecost.
        Weekdays in Time after Epiphany and Time after Trinity.

If several celebrations fall on the same day, the one that holds the highest rank according to the Table of Liturgical Days is observed. However, a Solemnity impeded by a liturgical day that takes precedence over it should be transferred to the closest day not listed under nos. 1-8 in the Table of Precedence, provided that what is laid down in no. 5 is observed. As to the Solemnity of the Annunciation of the Lord, whenever it falls on any day of Holy Week, it shall always be transferred to the Monday after the Second Sunday of Easter. Other celebrations are omitted in that year.

Should Evening Prayer of the current day's Office and First Evensong (Evening Prayer I) of the following day be assigned for celebration on the same day, then Evening Prayer of the celebration with the higher rank in the Table of Liturgical Days takes precedence; in cases of equal rank, Evening Prayer of the current day takes precedence.

3. *Special Days in the Life of the Ordinariate and its Communities*

(Some days on which a Solemn *Te Deum* of Thanksgiving may be appropriate. See DWM 1071)

1 Jan:	**Anniversary of the Erection of the Ordinariate of the Chair of Saint Peter** (2012)
2 Feb:	**Anniversary of the Episcopal Ordination of the Most Reverend Steven J. Lopes, First Bishop of the Ordinariate of the Chair of Saint Peter** (2016)
14 Feb:	**Anniversary of the Dedication of the Cathedral Church of the Ordinariate of the Chair of Saint Peter** (2004)
22 Feb:	**Chair of Saint Peter the Apostle** –Solemnity of Title of the Ordinariate of the Chair of Saint Peter
19 March:	**Saint Joseph, Spouse of the Blessed Virgin Mary** –Patronal Feastday of Canada
1 Sept:	**Our Lady of the Southern Cross** –Solemnity of Title of the Ordinariate of Our Lady of the Southern Cross in Australia
24 Sept:	**Our Lady of Walsingham** –Patronal Feast of the Ordinariate of the Chair of Saint Peter / Solemnity of Title of the Ordinariate of Our Lady of Walsingham in the United Kingdom / Solemnity of Title of the Cathedral Church of the Ordinariate of the Chair of Saint Peter
9 Oct:	**Saint John Henry Newman** –Patronal Feast of the Ordinariate of Our Lady of Walsingham in the United Kingdom
4 Nov:	**Anniversary of the Promulgation of the Apostolic Constitution *Anglicanorum coetibus*** (2009)
8 Dec:	**Immaculate Conception of the Blessed Virgin Mary** –Patronal Feastday of the United States of America

The Solemnity of Title of each parish: celebrated as a Solemnity and transferred, if allowed, to the adjacent, unimpeded Sunday according to the Table of Precedence

The Anniversary of the Dedication of each parish church: celebrated as a Solemnity and transferred, if allowed, to the adjacent, unimpeded Sunday according to the Table of Precedence

4. *Occasions when Mass texts of the day may be replaced*[1]

The following outline specifies when celebrations using the formularies from Ritual Masses, Masses for Various Needs and Occasions, Votive Masses, and Masses for the Dead are permitted within the liturgical year.

V1 = Ritual Masses (GIRM, no. 372).
Masses for Various Needs and Occasions and Votive Masses, in cases of serious need or pastoral advantage, at the direction of the Ordinary or with his permission (GIRM, no. 374).

V2 = Masses for Various Needs and Occasions and Votive Masses, in cases of serious need or pastoral advantage, at the discretion of the Pastor of the church or the Priest Celebrant (GIRM, no. 376). (The DWM provision for Masses of Saint Mary, celebrated over the liturgical year, constitutes a particular exception to this general norm in view of GIRM no. 378. See p. 6 of this Ordo, *above*).

V3 = Masses for Various Needs and Occasions and Votive Masses chosen by the Priest Celebrant in favor of the devotion of the people (GIRM, no. 373, 375).

D1 = Funeral Mass (GIRM, no. 380).

D2 = Mass on the occasion of news of a death, final burial, or the anniversary of death (GIRM, no. 381).

D3 = Daily Mass for the Dead (GIRM, no. 381). When D1 and D2 are not permitted, neither is D3.

$\sqrt{}$ = permitted.   ✗ = not permitted.

Liturgical days	V1	V2	V3	D1	D2	D3
1. Solemnities of precept (Holy Days of Obligation) 2. Sundays in the seasons of Advent, Lent, and Easter 3. Holy Thursday, Easter Triduum	✗	✗	✗	✗	✗	✗
4. Solemnities not of precept; All Souls' Day 5. Ash Wednesday; weekdays of Holy Week 6. Days in the Octave of Easter	✗	✗	✗	$\sqrt{}$	✗	✗
7. Sundays of Christmas and Sundays of Time after Epiphany and Trinitytide (Ordinary Time) 8. Feasts	$\sqrt{}$	✗	✗	$\sqrt{}$	✗	✗
9. Weekdays in the season of Advent from 17 to 24 December 10. Days in the Octave of Christmas 11. Days in Whitsun Week (Octave of Pentecost) 12. Weekdays in the season of Lent	$\sqrt{}$	✗	✗	$\sqrt{}$	$\sqrt{}$	✗
13. Obligatory memorials; Ember and Rogation Days 14. Weekdays in the season of Advent to 16 December 15. Weekdays in the season of Christmas from 2 January 16. Weekdays in the season of Easter	$\sqrt{}$	$\sqrt{}$	✗	$\sqrt{}$	$\sqrt{}$	✗
17. Weekdays in Time after Epiphany and Trinitytide (Ordinary Time)	$\sqrt{}$	$\sqrt{}$	$\sqrt{}$	$\sqrt{}$	$\sqrt{}$	$\sqrt{}$

---

[1] Cf. Table of Rubrics Governing Ritual Masses, Masses for Various Needs and Occasions, and Masses for the Dead, in *Ceremonial of Bishops* (1989), Appendix III (here adapted to the Ordinariate's Particular Calendar and the DWM Table of Precedence).

5. *Regarding "Ever One God" in the Divine Worship Collects*

In May 2020, the Congregation for Divine Worship wrote to the English-speaking conferences of bishops regarding the concluding doxology of the Collects in the Roman Missal. Specifically, the Congregation modified the English translation of the doxology, omitting the word "one" so that the conclusion now reads: *...through Jesus Christ, your Son our Lord, who lives and reigns with you, in the unity of the Holy Spirit, God for ever and ever*. This change was effective in the United States on Ash Wednesday, 2021, for all Masses celebrated in English according to the Roman Missal.

The change does ***not*** apply to Divine Worship.

On the one hand, the change in the translation of the Roman Missal brings the English into greater conformity with the Latin [...*Deus, per omnia saecula saeculorum*, not "unus Deus"]. But this is not simply a matter of strict adherence to the Latin but of liturgical logic, and hence the difference between the Roman and Anglican liturgical traditions.

Theologically, the logic of the Roman ending to the collect is meant to be understood in a Christological context...it is a statement about Christ's divinity: *Per Iesum Christum Filium tuum, qui vivet et regnat in unitate Spiritus Sancti, [qui est] Deus, per omnia sæcula sæculorum*. Grammatically, the Deus appears as a second modifier of Iesum after his living and reigning. So, the whole prayer is made through Christ, in the unity of the Holy Spirit. And ***about Christ,*** we add that (1) he is the Father's [your] Son; (2) that he lives and reigns with the Father in the communion of the Holy Spirit; and (3) and that this Jesus Christ is himself God for ever and ever.

The Anglican and Byzantine logic is different in that it is explicitly a Trinitarian affirmation. Having named the divine Persons, this logic then underscores the unicity of the Blessed Trinity as God. And it is noteworthy that this has been the case since the very first articulations of what we call now the Anglican liturgical tradition, since already the 1549 Prayer Book "doubles down" on the Trinitarian logic by adding *ever* one God.

Obviously these two readings of the conclusion of the Collect are not opposed or contradictory and can sit happily side-by-side. It is also a subtle and interesting example about how the Roman and Anglican logic differ, while each underscores an important aspect of the Mystery into which we have been baptized. Bottom line: when celebrating Mass according to the Roman Missal, it's "God, for ever and ever." When celebrating according to Divine Worship, it's "ever one God, world without end."

6. *Necrology*

Of your charity, recommend these our departed brothers to the seat of Divine Mercy:

The Rev. Lowell Andrews, October 3, 2018
The Rev. Michael Birch, November 26, 2016
The Rev. John Dale Cornelius, September 8, 2021
The Rev. Msgr. Laurence Gipson, July 29, 2021
The Rev. Lucien Lindsey, Jr., March 19, 2018

Made in the USA
Las Vegas, NV
08 April 2024

88439227R00070